Hands-On Design Patterns with Kotlin

Build scalable applications using traditional, reactive, and concurrent design patterns in Kotlin

Alexey Soshin

BIRMINGHAM - MUMBAI

Hands-On Design Patterns with Kotlin

Commissioning Editor: Richa Tripathi
Acquisition Editor: Shriram Shekhar
Content Development Editor: Zeeyan Pinheiro
Technical Editor: Ketan Kamble
Copy Editor: Safis Editing
Project Coordinator: Vaidehi Sawant
Proofreader: Safis Editing
Indexer: Rekha Nair
Graphics: Jason Monteiro
Production Coordinator: Aparna Bhagat

First published: June 2018

Production reference: 1130618

Published by Packt Publishing Ltd.
Livery Place
35 Livery Street
Birmingham
B3 2PB, UK.

ISBN 978-1-78899-801-7

www.packtpub.com

To Lula Leus, my constant source of inspiration.

To my mentor, Lior Bar On. Without you, I would have never started writing.

`mapt.io`

Mapt is an online digital library that gives you full access to over 5,000 books and videos, as well as industry leading tools to help you plan your personal development and advance your career. For more information, please visit our website.

Why subscribe?

- Spend less time learning and more time coding with practical eBooks and Videos from over 4,000 industry professionals

- Improve your learning with Skill Plans built especially for you

- Get a free eBook or video every month

- Mapt is fully searchable

- Copy and paste, print, and bookmark content

PacktPub.com

Did you know that Packt offers eBook versions of every book published, with PDF and ePub files available? You can upgrade to the eBook version at `www.PacktPub.com` and as a print book customer, you are entitled to a discount on the eBook copy. Get in touch with us at `service@packtpub.com` for more details.

At `www.PacktPub.com`, you can also read a collection of free technical articles, sign up for a range of free newsletters, and receive exclusive discounts and offers on Packt books and eBooks.

Contributors

About the author

Alexey Soshin is a software architect with 13 years of experience of making software, mostly for JVM. He started exploring Kotlin even before Kotlin 1.0 was released, and since then, he has been a big enthusiast of the language. He speaks about Kotlin and reactive frameworks at various conferences and meetups and maintains a technical blog. He's also a contributor to Vert.x, a toolkit for building reactive applications on the Java Virtual Machine.

About the reviewers

Ranga Rao Karanam is a programmer, trainer, and architect. He is the founder of in28Minutes—helping 200,000 learners reskill on Cloud native applications, microservices, evolutionary design, high-quality code, DevOps, BDD, TDD, and refactoring. He loves consulting for startups on the development of scalable component-based cloud-native applications and following modern development practices, such as BDD, continuous delivery, and DevOps.

Ranga likes to play cricket and tennis, and he is a regular hiker. His dream is to spend a year hiking in the Himalayas.

Ganesh Samarthyam is a co-founder of CodeOps Technologies, a software technology, consultancy, and training company based in Bangalore. He has 16 years of experience in the IT industry, and his latest book, *Refactoring for Software Design Smells* by Morgan Kaufmann/Elsevier, has been translated into Korean and Chinese. Ganesh loves exploring anything and everything about technology in his free time.

Packt is searching for authors like you

If you're interested in becoming an author for Packt, please visit `authors.packtpub.com` and apply today. We have worked with thousands of developers and tech professionals, just like you, to help them share their insight with the global tech community. You can make a general application, apply for a specific hot topic that we are recruiting an author for, or submit your own idea.

Table of Contents

Preface

Design patterns enable you as a developer to speed up the development process by providing tested, proven development paradigms. Reusing design patterns helps prevent complex issues that can cause major problems and improves your code base, promotes code reuse, and makes the architecture more robust.

The mission of this book is to ease the adoption of design patterns in Kotlin and provide good practices for programmers.

The book begins by showing you the practical aspects of smarter coding in Kotlin, explaining the basic Kotlin syntax and the impact of design patterns. Furthermore, the book provides an in-depth explanation of the classic design patterns, such as Creational, Structural, and Behavioral, before heading into functional programming. It then takes you through Reactive and Concurrent patterns, teaching you about Streams, Threads, and Coroutines to write better code. Toward the end, you will learn about the latest trends in architecture, exploring the design patterns for microservices, and discuss the considerations when choosing between different architectures, such as microservices and MVC.

By the end of the book, you will be able to efficiently address common problems faced while developing applications and be comfortable working on scalable and maintainable projects of any size.

Who this book is for

This book is for developers who would like to master design patterns with Kotlin in order to build efficient and scalable applications. Basic Java or Kotlin programming knowledge is assumed.

What this book covers

Chapter 1, *Getting Started with Kotlin*, covers basic language concepts and syntax, such as types, functions, classes, and flow control structures.

Chapter 2, *Working with Creational Patterns*, explains what classical creational patterns are embedded into the language and how to implement those that aren't. It discusses Singleton and Factory, among others.

Chapter 3, *Understanding Structural Patterns*, focuses on how to extend the functionality of our objects and adapt to changes.

Chapter 4, *Getting Familiar with Behavioral Patterns*, explains how can we alter object behavior at runtime, iteration over complex data structures, and communication between objects using the Observable design pattern.

Chapter 5, *Functional Programming*, dives into the principles of functional programming and how they fit into Kotlin. Topics such as data immutability and functions as a first-class value will be discussed in depth.

Chapter 6, *Streaming Your Data*, shows how applying the principles of functional programming help us process potentially infinite streams of incoming data.

Chapter 7, *Staying Reactive*, explains what reactive principles are and gives extensive examples based on the Reactive Extensions framework, better known as simply Rx.

Chapter 8, *Threads and Coroutines*, shows how easy it to work with concurrent code in Kotlin, making use of its lightweight thread model.

Chapter 9, *Designed for Concurrency*, covers design patterns that help us process many tasks at the same time, using coroutines.

Chapter 10, *Idioms and Anti-Patterns*, provides guidelines on some best practices and pitfalls that you may encounter while developing in Kotlin.

Chapter 11, *Reactive Microservices with Kotlin*, goes over a detailed example of writing a microservice using Kotlin, Vert.x, and PostgreSQL.

To get the most out of this book

In this book, we assume that the reader has basic knowledge of Java programming language and what JVM is.

It is also assumed that the reader is comfortable working with the command line.

A few command-line examples we use in this book are based on OSX, but could be easily adapted for Windows or Linux.

Download the example code files

You can download the example code files for this book from your account at www.packtpub.com. If you purchased this book elsewhere, you can visit www.packtpub.com/support and register to have the files emailed directly to you.

You can download the code files by following these steps:

1. Log in or register at www.packtpub.com.
2. Select the **SUPPORT** tab.
3. Click on **Code Downloads & Errata**.
4. Enter the name of the book in the **Search** box and follow the onscreen instructions.

Once the file is downloaded, please make sure that you unzip or extract the folder using the latest version of:

- WinRAR/7-Zip for Windows
- Zipeg/iZip/UnRarX for Mac
- 7-Zip/PeaZip for Linux

The code bundle for the book is also hosted on GitHub at https://github.com/PacktPublishing/Hands-on-Design-Patterns-with-Kotlin. In case there's an update to the code, it will be updated on the existing GitHub repository.

We also have other code bundles from our rich catalog of books and videos available at https://github.com/PacktPublishing/. Check them out!

Conventions used

There are a number of text conventions used throughout this book.

CodeInText: Indicates code words in text, database table names, folder names, filenames, file extensions, pathnames, dummy URLs, user input, and Twitter handles. Here is an example: "Kotlin's extension is usually .kt."

A block of code is set as follows:

```
var s = "I'm a string"
s = 1 // s is a String
```

When we wish to draw your attention to a particular part of a code block, the relevant lines or items are set in bold:

```
var s = "I'm a string"
s = 1 // s is a String
```

Any command-line input or output is written as follows:

```
I would suggest: a guitar
```

Bold: Indicates a new term, an important word, or words that you see onscreen. For example, words in menus or dialog boxes appear in the text like this. Here is an example: "One of the most common tasks for Java developers is to create another **Plain Old Java Object (POJO)**."

 Warnings or important notes appear like this.

 Tips and tricks appear like this.

Get in touch

Feedback from our readers is always welcome.

General feedback: Email feedback@packtpub.com and mention the book title in the subject of your message. If you have questions about any aspect of this book, please email us at questions@packtpub.com.

Errata: Although we have taken every care to ensure the accuracy of our content, mistakes do happen. If you have found a mistake in this book, we would be grateful if you would report this to us. Please visit www.packtpub.com/submit-errata, selecting your book, clicking on the Errata Submission Form link, and entering the details.

Piracy: If you come across any illegal copies of our works in any form on the Internet, we would be grateful if you would provide us with the location address or website name. Please contact us at copyright@packtpub.com with a link to the material.

If you are interested in becoming an author: If there is a topic that you have expertise in and you are interested in either writing or contributing to a book, please visit authors.packtpub.com.

Reviews

Please leave a review. Once you have read and used this book, why not leave a review on the site that you purchased it from? Potential readers can then see and use your unbiased opinion to make purchase decisions, we at Packt can understand what you think about our products, and our authors can see your feedback on their book. Thank you!

For more information about Packt, please visit packtpub.com.

Getting Started with Kotlin

1

In this chapter, we'll cover basic Kotlin syntax, and discuss what design patterns are good for and why they should be used in Kotlin.

The goal of this chapter is not to cover the entire language vocabulary, but to get you familiar with some basic concepts and idioms. The following chapters will slowly expose you to more language features as they become relevant to the design patterns we'll discuss.

In this chapter, we will cover the following topics:

- Basic language syntax and features
- Introduction to design patterns

Basic language syntax and features

Whether you come from Java, C#, Scala or any other statically typed programming language, you'll find Kotlin syntax quite familiar. This is not by coincidence, but to make the transfer to this new language as smooth as possible for those with previous experience in other languages. Besides that familiarity, Kotlin brings a vast amount of features, such as better type safety. As we move ahead, you'll notice that all of them are attempting to solve real-world problems. That pragmatic approach is very consistent across the language. For example, one of the strongest sides of Kotlin is complete Java interoperability. You can have Java and Kotlin classes alongside each other, and freely use any library that is available in Java for a Kotlin project.

To summarize, the goals of language are as follows:

- Pragmatism
- Having clear syntax
- Being type-safe
- Interoperability

The first chapter will discuss how these goals are achieved.

Multi-paradigm

Some of the major paradigms in programming languages are procedural, object-oriented, and functional paradigms.

Being practical, Kotlin allows for any of these paradigms. It has classes and inheritance, coming from the object-oriented approach. It has higher-order functions from functional programming. But you don't have to wrap everything in classes if you don't want to. You can structure your entire code as just a set of procedures and structs. You will see how all these approaches come together, as different examples will use different paradigms to solve the problems discussed.

Code structure

The first thing you'll need to do when you start programming in Kotlin is create a new file. Kotlin's extension is usually `.kt`.

Unlike Java, there's no strong relationship between the filename and class name. You can put as many public classes in your file as you want, as long as the classes are related to one another and your file doesn't grow too long to read.

No semicolons

In Java, every line of code must be terminated with a semicolon:

```
System.out.println("Hello"); //<- This is a semicolon
System.out.println("World"); //<- I still see you, semicolon
```

But Kotlin is a pragmatic language. So, instead, it infers during compilation where it should put the semicolons:

```
println("Hello") //<- No semicolon here
println("World") //<- Not here
```

Most of the time, you won't need to put semicolons in your code. They're considered optional.

Naming conventions

As a convention, if your file contains a single class, name your file the same as your class.

If your file contains more than one class, then the filename should describe the common purpose of those classes. Use CamelCase when naming your files, as per the Kotlin Coding Conventions: `https://kotlinlang.org/docs/reference/coding-conventions.html#naming-rules`.

 Actually, you don't have to write your code in a file for simple snippets. You can also play with the language online: try `http://kotlinlang.org/` or use REPL and interactive shell after installing Kotlin and running `kotlinc`.

Packages

It wouldn't be convenient to have all your classes and functions in the same folder or under the same namespace. That's the reason Kotlin, similar to many other languages, uses the notion of a package.

Like Java, Kotlin uses packages:

```
package me.soshin.controllers
```

If you're mixing Java and Kotlin, Kotlin files should follow Java package rules.

In purely Kotlin projects, common package prefixes can be omitted from the folder structure. For example, if all your projects are under the `me.soshin` package, place your controllers in the `/controllers` folder and not in the `/me/soshin/controllers` folder like Java does.

Types

We'll start with the Kotlin type system, and compare it to what Java provides.

 The Java examples are for familiarity, and not to prove that Kotlin is superior to Java in any way.

Type inference

Let's define a simple string in Java:

```
String s = "Hello World";
```

We defined that `s` is of type `String`. But why? Isn't it obvious at this point?

Kotlin provides us with type inference:

```
val s = "Hello World"
```

Now, the compiler will decide what type of variable should be used. Unlike interpreted languages (such as JavaScript, Groovy, or Ruby), the type of variable is defined only once. This will not work:

```
var s = "I'm a string"
s = 1 // s is a String
```

You may wonder why we've used one `var` and one `val` to define the variables. We'll explain it shortly.

val versus var

In Java, variables can be declared final. Final variables can be assigned only once:

```
final String s = "Hi";
s = "Bye"; // Doesn't work
```

Kotlin urges you to use immutable data as much as possible. Final variables in Kotlin are simply `val`:

```
val s = "Hi"
s = "Bye" // Doesn't work
```

If you do have a case in which you would like to reassign a variable, use `var` instead:

```
var s = "Hi"
s = "Bye" // Works now
```

Comparison

We were taught very early in Java that comparing objects using `==` won't produce the expected results, since it tests for reference equality, and we need to use `equals()` for that.

JVM does string interning to prevent that in some basic cases, so for the sake of the example we'll use `new String()` to avoid that:

```
String s1 = "ABC";
String s2 = new String(s1);

System.out.println(s1 == s2); // false
```

Kotlin translates `==` to `equals()`:

```
val s1 = "ABC"
val s2 = String(s1.toCharArray())

println(s1 == s2) // true
```

If you do want to check for reference equality, use `===`:

```
println(s1 === s2) // false
```

Null safety

Probably the most notorious exception in the Java world is `NullPointerException`.

The reason behind this exception is that every object in Java can be `null`. The code here shows us why:

```
String s = "Hello";
...
s = null;
System.out.println(s.length); // Causes NullPointerException
```

In this case, marking `s` as `final` would prevent the exception.

But what about this one:

```
public class Printer {
    public static void printLength(final String s) {
        System.out.println(s.length);
    }
}
```

From anywhere in the code it's still possible to pass `null`:

```
Printer.printLength(null); // Again, NullPointerException
```

Since Java 8, there's been an `optional` construct:

```
if (optional.isPresent()) {
    System.out.println(optional.get());
}
```

In a more functional style:

```
optional.ifPresent(System.out::println);
```

But... it doesn't solve our problem. We can still pass `null` instead of the proper `Optional.empty()` and crash the program.

Kotlin checks it even earlier—during compile time:

```
val s : String = null // Won't compile
```

Let's go back to our `printLength()` function:

```
fun printLength(s: String) {
    println(s.length)
}
```

Calling this function with null won't compile any more:

```
printLength(null) // Null can not be a value of a non-null type String
```

If you specifically want your type to be able to receive nulls, you'll need to mark it as nullable using the question mark:

```
val notSoSafe : String? = null
```

Declaring functions

Everything is an object in Java. If you have a method that doesn't rely on any state, it still must be wrapped by a class. You're probably familiar with a lot of `Util` classes in Java that only have static methods, and their only purpose is to satisfy the language requirements and bundle those methods together.

In Kotlin, a function can be declared outside of a class instead of the following code:

```
public class MyFirstClass {
```

```java
public static void main(String[] args) {
    System.out.println("Hello world");
}
}
```

It's enough to have:

```kotlin
fun main(args: Array<String>) {
    println("Hello, world!")
}
```

Functions declared outside of any class are already static.

 Many examples in this book assume that the code we provide is wrapped in the main function. If you don't see a signature of the function, it probably should be:
`fun main(args: Array<String>)`.

The keyword to declare a function is `fun`. The argument type comes after the argument name, and not before. And if the function doesn't return anything, the return type can be omitted completely.

What if you do want to declare the return type? Again, it will come after the function declaration:

```kotlin
fun getGreeting(): String {
    return "Hello, world!"
}

fun main(args: Array<String>) {
    println(getGreeting())
}
```

There are lots of other topics regarding function declarations, such as default and named arguments, default parameters, and variable numbers of arguments. We'll introduce them in the following chapters, with relevant examples.

Control flow

One could say that control flow is the bread and butter of writing programs. We'll start with two conditional expressions: `if` and `when`.

Using the if expression

Previously it was noted that Kotin likes variables to be assigned only once. And it also doesn't like nulls so much. You probably wondered how that would ever work out in the real world. In Java, constructs such as this are quite common:

```
public String getUnixSocketPolling(boolean isBsd) {
    String value = null;
    if (isBsd) {
        value = "kqueue";
    }
    else {
        value = "epoll";
    }

    return value;
}
```

Of course, this is an oversimplified situation, but still, you have a variable that at some point absolutely must be `null`, right?

In Java, `if` is just a statement and doesn't return anything. On the contrary, in Kotlin, `if` is an expression, meaning it returns a value:

```
fun getUnixSocketPolling(isBsd : Boolean) : String {
    val value = if (isBsd) {
        "kqueue"
    } else {
        "epoll"
    }
    return value
}
```

If you are familiar with Java, you can easily read this code. This function receives a Boolean (which cannot be null), and returns a string (and never a null). But since it is an expression, it can return a result. And the result is assigned to our variable only once.

We can simplify it even further:

1. The return type could be inferred
2. The return as the last line can be omitted
3. A simple `if` expression can be written in one line

So, our final result in Kotlin will look like this:

```
fun getUnixSocketPolling(isBsd : Boolean) = if (isBsd) "kqueue" else
"epoll"
```

Single line functions in Kotlin are very cool and pragmatic. But you should make sure that somebody else other than you can understand what they do. Use with care.

Using the when expression

What if (no pun intended) we want to have more conditions in our `if` statement?

In Java, we use the `switch` statement. In Kotlin, there's a `when` expression, which is a lot more powerful, since it can embed some other Kotlin features.

Let's create a method that's based on the amount of money that will give cause to suggest a nice birthday gift:

```
fun suggestGift(amount : Int) : String {
    return when (amount) {
        in (0..10) -> "a book"
        in (10..100) -> "a guitar"
        else -> if (amount < 0) "no gift" else "anything!"
    }
}
```

As you can see, `when` also supports a range of values. The default case is covered by the `else` block. In the following examples, we will elaborate on even more powerful ways to use this expression.

As a general rule, use `when` if you have more than two conditions. Use `if` for simple checks.

String interpolation

What if we would like to actually print those results?

First, as you may have already noticed, in one of the examples above, Kotlin provides a nifty `println()` standard function that wraps the bulkier `System.out.println()` from Java.

But, more importantly, as in many other modern languages, Kotlin supports string interpolation using the `${}` syntax. Following on from the example before:

```
println("I would suggest: ${suggestGift(10)} ")
```

The preceding code would print:

I would suggest: a book

If you're interpolating a variable, and not a function, curly braces could be omitted:

```
val gift = suggestGift(100)
println("I would suggest: $gift ")
```

This would print the following output:

I would suggest: a guitar

Classes and inheritance

Although Kotlin is multi-paradigm, it has a strong affinity to the Java programming language, which is based on classes. Keeping Java and JVM interoperability in mind, it's no wonder that Kotlin also has the notion of classes and classical inheritance.

Classes

To declare a `class`, we use a class keyword, exactly like in Java:

```
class Player {
}
```

There's no `new` keyword in Kotlin. The instantiation of a class simply looks like this:

```
// Kotlin figured out you want to create a new player
val p = Player()
```

If the class has no body, as in this simple example, we can omit the **curly brackets**:

```
class Player // Totally fine
```

Inheritance

Exactly like in Java, abstract classes are marked by `abstract` and interfaces by
the `interface` keyword:

```kotlin
abstract class AbstractDungeonMaster {
    abstract val gameName: String

    fun startGame() {
        println("Game $gameName has started!")
    }
}


interface Dragon
```

As in Java 8, interfaces in Kotlin can have a default implementation of functions, as long as
they don't rely on any state:

```kotlin
interface Greeter {
    fun sayHello() {
        println("Hello")
    }
}
```

There are no `inherits` and `implements` keywords in Kotlin. Instead, both the name of an
abstract class and all the names of the interfaces that class implements are put after a colon:

```kotlin
class DungeonMaster: Greeter, AbstractDungeonMaster() {
    override val gameName: String
        get() = "Dungeon of the Beholder"
}
```

We can still distinguish the abstract class by the parenthesis that comes after its name, and
there can still be only one `abstract` class, as there are no multiple inheritances in Kotlin.

Our `DungeonMaster` has access to both functions from `Greeter` and
`AbstractDungeonMaster`:

```kotlin
val p = DungeonMaster()
p.sayHello()  // From Greeter interface
p.startGame() // From AbstractDungeonMaster abstract class
```

Calling the preceding code, it will print the following output:

```
Hello
Game Dungeon of the Beholder has started!
```

Constructors

Our `DungeonMaster` looks a bit awkward now, since it can proclaim the start of only one game. Let's add a non-empty constructor to our `abstract` class to fix that:

```
abstract class AbstractDungeonMaster(private val gameName : String) {
    fun startGame() {
        println("Game $gameName has started!")
    }
}
```

Now, our `DungeonMaster` must receive the name of the game and pass it to the `abstract` class:

```
open class DungeonMaster(gameName: String):
        Greeter, AbstractDungeonMaster(gameName)
```

What if we wanted to extend `DungeonMaster` by having an `EvilDungeonMaster`?

In Java, all classes can be extended, unless they're marked `final`. In Kotlin, no class can be extended, unless it's marked `open`. The same goes for functions in abstract classes. That's the reason why we declared `DungeonMaster` as `open` in the first place.

We'll change `AbstractDungeonMaster` a bit again to give more power to the evil ruler:

```
open fun startGame() {
    // Everything else stays the same
}
```

Now, we add the following to our `EvilDungeonMaster` implementation:

```
class EvilDungeonMaster(private val awfulGame: String) :
DungeonMaster(awfulGame) {
    override fun sayHello() {
        println("Prepare to die! Muwahaha!!!")
    }

    override fun startGame() {
        println("$awfulGame will be your last!")
    }
}
```

Whereas in Java, `@Override` is an optional annotation, in Kotlin it is a mandatory keyword.

You cannot hide supertype methods, and code that doesn't use `override` explicitly won't compile.

Properties

In Java, we are used to the concept of getters and setters. A typical class may look something like this:

```
public class Person {
    private String name;

    public String getName() {
        return name;
    }

    public void setName(String name) {
        this.name = name;
    }

    // More methods come here
}
```

If we want to get a person's name, we call `getName()`. If we want to change it, we call `setName()`. That's quite simple.

If we want to set the name only once, during object instantiation, we can specify the non-default constructor and remove the setter as follows:

```
public class ImmutablePerson {
    private String name;

    public ImmutablePerson(String name) {
        this.name = name;
    }

    public String getName() {
        return name;
    }
}
```

All this dates back to the beginning of Java, somewhere around '95.

But if you've worked with C#, for example, you're probably familiar with the idea of properties. To understand them, let's go to the first example and change it a bit:

```
public class PublicPerson {
    public String name;
}
```

Reading a person's name is not much shorter: `p.name`.

Also, changing the name is much more intuitive: `p.name = "Alex";`.

But by doing so, we lost a lot of control over our object. We cannot make `PublicPerson` immutable. If we want everybody to be able to read the person's name, they'll also be able to change it at any point in time. And what if later we decide that all names must be uppercase? With setter, we could do that. But not with the public field.

Properties provide a solution for all those problems:

```
class Person() {
    var name : String = ""
}
```

This may look the same as the Java example, with all its problems. But actually, behind the scenes, it's compiled to a getter and setter pair, just like the first example.

And since properties in Kotlin are translated into getters and setters, we can also control their behavior:

```
class Person {
    var name : String = ""
    set(value) {
        field = value.toUpperCase()
    }
}
```

Note that we don't need to check that `value` is null. The `String` type simply cannot receive nulls.

Coming from Java, it may seem intuitive to use the following assignment: `this.name = value.toUpperCase()`. But, in Kotlin, this will create a circular dependency. Instead, there's a `field` identifier that we're using, which is provided automatically.

Data classes

Remember how Kotlin is all about productiveness? One of the most common tasks for Java developers is to create another **Plain Old Java Object** (**POJO**). If you're not familiar with POJO, it is basically an object that only has getters, setters, and an implementation of `equals` or `hashCode` methods.

This task is so common that Kotlin has it built into the language:

```
data class User (val username : String, val password : String)
```

This will generate a class with two getters and no setters (note the `val` part), which will also implement `equals`, `hashCode`, and `clone` functions in the correct way.

The introduction of data classes is one of the biggest improvements in reducing the amount of boilerplate in the language.

More control flow – loops

Now let's discuss another common control structure—a loop. Loops are a very natural construct for most developers. Without loops, it would be very hard to repeat the same block of code more than once (although we will discuss how to do that without loops in later chapters).

The for loop

The `for` loop in Java, which prints each character of a string on a new line, may look something like this:

```
final String word = "Word";
for (int i = 0; i < word.length; i++) {
}
```

The same loop in Kotlin is:

```
val word = "Word";
for (i in 0..(word.length-1)) {
    println(word[i])
}
```

Note that while the usual `for` loop in Java is exclusive (it excludes the last index by definition, unless specified otherwise), the `for` loop over ranges in Kotlin is inclusive. That's the reason we have to subtract one from the length to prevent overflow (string index out of range): `(word.length-1)`.

If you want to avoid that, you can use the `until` function:

```
val word = "Word";
for (i in 0 until word.length) {
    println(word[i])
}
```

Unlike some other languages, reversing the range indexes won't work:

```
val word = "Word";
for (i in (word.length-1)..0) {
    println(word[i])
} // Doesn't print anything
```

If your intention is to print the word in reverse order, for example, use the `downTo` function:

```
val word = "Word";
for (i in (word.length-1) downTo 0) {
    println(word[i])
}
```

It will print the following output:

```
d
r
o
W
```

It may seem confusing that `until` and `downTo` are called functions, although they look more like operators. This is another interesting Kotlin feature called **infix call**, which will be discussed later on.

For-each loop

Of course, if you're a bit familiar with Java, you may argue that the previous code could be improved by using a `for-each` construct instead:

```
final String word = "Word";
```

```
for (Character c : word.toCharArray()) {
    System.out.println(c);
}
```

The same in Kotlin would be:

```
val word = "Word"

for (c in word) {
    println(c)
}
```

While loop

There are no changes to the `while` loop functionality, so we'll cover them very briefly:

```
var x = 0
while (x < 10) {
    x++
    println(x)
}
```

This will print numbers from 1 to 10. Note that we are forced to define x as `var`. In the following chapters, we'll discuss much more idiomatic ways to do this.

The lesser used `do while` loop is also present in the language:

```
var x = 5
    do {
        println(x)
        x--
} while (x > 0)
```

Extension functions

You may have noticed from the previous examples that `String` in Kotlin has some methods that its Java counterpart is lacking, such as `reversed()`. How is that achieved, if it's the same `String` type as in Java and, as we know, `String` in Java cannot be extended by any other class, since it's declared `final`?

If you look at the source code, you'll find the following:

```
public inline fun String.reversed(): String {
    return (this as CharSequence).reversed().toString()
}
```

This feature is called an extension function, and it also exists in some other languages, such as C# or Groovy.

To extend a class without inheriting from it, we prefix the function name, `reversed` in our example, with a class name we want to extend.

Do note that the extension function cannot override the member function. The `inline` keyword will be discussed in later chapters.

Introduction to design patterns

Now that we are a bit familiar with basic Kotlin syntax, we can move on to discuss what design patterns are all about.

What are design patterns?

There are different misconceptions surrounding design patterns. In general, they are as follows:

- Missing language features
- Not necessary in dynamic language
- Relevant only to object-oriented languages
- Relevant only to enterprises

But actually, design patterns are just a proven way to solve a common problem. As a concept, they are not limited to a specific programming language (Java), nor to a family of languages (C-family, for example), nor are they limited to programming in general. You may have even heard of design patterns in software architecture, which discuss how different systems can efficiently communicate with each other. There are service-oriented architectural patterns, which you may know as **Service-Oriented Architecture (SOA)**, and microservice design patterns that evolved from SOA and emerged over the past few years. The future will, for sure, bring us even more design pattern *families*.

Even in the physical world, outside software development, we're surrounded by design patterns and commonly accepted solutions to a certain problem. Let's look at an example.

Design patterns in real life

Did you ride an elevator lately? Was there a mirror on the wall of the elevator? Why is that?

How did you feel when you last rode an elevator that had no mirror and no glass walls?

The main reason we commonly have mirrors in our elevators is to solve a common problem. Riding in an elevator is boring. We could put in a picture. But a picture would also get boring after a while, if you rode the same elevator at least twice a day. Cheap, but not much of an improvement.

We could put in a TV screen, as some do. But it makes the elevator more expensive. And it also requires a lot of maintenance. We need to put some content on the screen, to make it not too repetitive. So either there's a person whose responsibility is to renew the content once in a while, or a third-party company that does it for us. We'll also have to handle different problems that may occur with screen hardware and the software behind it. Seeing the "Blue Screen of Death" is amusing, of course, but only mildly.

Some architects even go for putting elevator shafts on the building exterior, and making part of the walls transparent. This may provide some exciting views. But this solution also requires maintenance (dirty windows don't make for the best view), and a lot of architectural planning.

So, we put in a mirror. You get to watch an attractive person even if you ride alone. Some studies indicate that we find ourselves more attractive than we are, anyway. Maybe you get a chance to review your appearances one last time before that important meeting. Mirrors visually expand the visual space and make the entire trip less claustrophobic, or less awkward, if it's the start of a day and the elevator is really crowded.

Design process

Let's try and understand what we did just now.

We didn't invent mirrors in elevators. We've seen them thousands of times. But we formalized the problem (riding in an elevator is boring) and discussed alternative solutions (TV screens, glass walls) and the benefits of the commonly used solution (solves the problem, easy to implement). That's what design patterns are all about.

The basic steps of the design process are:

1. Define exactly what the current problem is.
2. Consider different alternatives, based on the pros and cons.
3. Choose the solution that solves the problem, while best fitting your specific constraints.

Why use design patterns in Kotlin?

Kotlin comes to solve the real-world problems of today. In the following chapters, we will discuss both *Design Patterns* first introduced by the Gang of Four back in '94, as well as design patterns that emerged from the functional programming paradigm.

You'll find that some of the design patterns are so common or useful that they're already built into the language as reserved keywords or standard functions. Some of them will need to combine a set of language features. And some are not so useful any more, since the world has moved forward, and they're being replaced by some other patterns.

But in any case, familiarity with design patterns and best practices expands your "developer toolbox" and creates shared vocabulary between you and your colleagues.

Summary

So, in this chapter, we covered the main goals of the Kotlin programming language.

We went through the variables that are defined, such as `val`, `var`, null safety, and type inference. We observed how program flow is controlled by commands such as `if`, `when`, `for`, and `while`, and we also took a look at the different keywords used to define classes and interfaces: `class`, `interface`, `data`, and `abstract` class. We learned how to construct new classes and how we inherit from interfaces and implement classes. And finally, we learned what design patterns are good for, and why we need them in Kotlin.

In the next chapter, we'll start discussing the first of the three design pattern families: creation patterns.

2
Working with Creational Patterns

In this chapter, we'll cover how classical creational patterns are implemented in Kotlin. These patterns deal with *how* and *when* you create your objects. Mastering these patterns will allow you to manage your objects better, adapt well to changes, and write code that is easy to maintain.

In this chapter, we will cover the following topics:

- Singleton
- Factory Method
- Abstract Factory
- Builder
- Prototype

Singleton

This is the most popular single guy in the neighborhood. Everybody knows him, everybody talks about him, and anybody can find him easily.

Even people who will frown when other design patterns are mentioned will know it by name. At some point, it was even proclaimed an anti-pattern, but only because of its wide popularity. So, for those who are hearing about it for the first time, what is this pattern about?

Usually, if you have an object, you can create as many of its instances as you want. Say, for example, you have the `Cat` class:

```
class Cat
```

You can produce as many of its instances (cats, to be precise), as you want:

```
val firstCat = Cat()
val secondCat = Cat()
val yetAnotherCat = Cat()
```

And there's no problem with that.

What if we wanted to disallow such behavior? Clearly, we have to create an object in some way for the first time. But from the second time on, we need to recognize that this object was initialized once already, and returns its instance instead. That's the main idea behind being a Singleton.

In Java and some other languages, this task is quite complex. It's not enough to simply make the constructor private and *remember* that the object was initialized at least once already. We also need to prevent race conditions, where two separate threads try to initialize it exactly at the same time. If we allowed that, it would break the entire concept of a Singleton, as two threads would hold references to two instances of the same object.

Solving this problem in Java requires doing one of the following:

- Accepting that a Singleton will initialize eagerly when your application starts, and not when it is first accessed
- Writing some smart code to prevent such race conditions and still stay performant
- Using a framework that already solves it

Kotlin just introduces a reserved keyword for that. Behold, an object as follows:

```
object MySingelton{}
```

 You don't need curly brackets there. They're just for visual consistency.

This combines declaration and initialization in one keyword. From now on, `MySingleton` can be accessed from anywhere in your code, and there'll be exactly one instance of it.

Of course, this object doesn't do anything interesting. Let's make it count the number of invocations instead:

```
object CounterSingleton {
    private val counter = AtomicInteger(0)
```

```
    fun increment() = counter.incrementAndGet()
}
```

We won't test it for thread safety yet this is a topic that will be covered in Chapter 8, *Threads and Coroutines*, which deals with threads. For now, we test it only to see how we call our Singleton:

```
for (i in 1..10) {
    println(CounterSingleton.increment())
}
```

This will print numbers between 1 and 10, as expected. As you can see, we don't need the getInstance() method at all.

 The object keyword is used for more than just creating Singletons. We'll discuss it in depth later.

Objects can't have constructors. If you want some kind of initialization logic for your Singleton, such as loading data from the database or over the network for the first time, you can use the init block instead:

```
object CounterSingleton {

    init {
        println("I was accessed for the first time")
    }
    // More code goes here
}
```

It is also demonstrated that Singletons in Kotlin are initialized lazily, and not eagerly, as some could suspect from the ease of their declaration. Just like regular classes, objects can extend other classes and implement interfaces. We'll come back to this in Chapter 10, *Idioms and Anti-Patterns*.

Factory Method

The Factory Method is all about creating objects. But why do we need a method to create objects? Isn't it what constructors are all about?

Well, constructors have their inherent limitations, which we're about to discuss.

Factory

We'll start with the Factory Method formalized in the book *Design Patterns* by Gang of Four.

This is one of the first patterns I teach my students. They're usually very anxious about the whole concept of design patterns, since it has an aura of mystery and complexity. So, what I do is ask them the following question.

Assume you have some class declaration, for example:

```
class Cat {
    val name = "Cat"
}
```

Could you write a function that returns a new instance of the class? Most of them would succeed:

```
fun catFactory() : Cat {
    return Cat()
}
```

Check that everything works:

```
val c = catFactory()
println(c.name) // Indeed prints "Cat"
```

Well, that's really simple, right?

Now, based on the argument we provide it, can this method create one of two objects?

Let's say we now have a Dog:

```
class Dog {
    val name = "Dog"
}
```

Choosing between two types of objects to instantiate would require only passing an argument:

```
fun animalFactory(animalType: String) : Cat {
    return Cat()
}
```

Of course, we can't always return a Cat now. So we create a common interface to be returned:

```
interface Animal {
```

```
    val name : String
}
```

What's left is to use the when expression to return an instance of the correct class:

```
return when (animalType.toLowerCase()) {
    "cat" -> Cat()
    "dog" -> Dog()
    else -> throw RuntimeException("Unknown animal $animalType")
}
```

That's what Factory Method is all about:

- Get some value.
- Return one of the objects that implement the common interface.

This pattern is very useful when creating objects from a configuration. Imagine we have a text file with the following contents that came from a veterinary clinic:

```
dog, dog, cat, dog, cat, cat
```

Now we would like to create an empty profile for each animal. Assuming we've already read the file contents and split them into a list, we can do the following:

```
val animalTypes = listOf("dog", "dog", "cat", "dog", "cat", "cat")
for (t in animalTypes) {
  val c = animalFactory(t)
    println(c.name)
}
```

 listOf is a function that comes from the Kotlin standard library that creates an immutable list of provided objects.

If your Factory Method doesn't need to have a state, we can leave it as a function.

But what if we want to assign a unique sequential identifier for each animal? Take a look at the following code block:

```
interface Animal {
    val id : Int
    // Same as before
}

class Cat(override val id: Int) : Animal {
    // Same as before
}
```

```
class Dog(override val id: Int) : Animal {
    // Same as before
}
```

Note that we can override values inside the constructor.

Our factory becomes a proper class now:

```
class AnimalFactory {
    var counter = 0
    fun createAnimal(animalType: String) : Animal {
        return when (animalType.trim().toLowerCase()) {
            "cat" -> Cat(++counter)
            "dog" -> Dog(++counter)
            else -> throw RuntimeException("Unknown animal $animalType")
        }
    }
}
```

So we'll have to initialize it:

```
val factory = AnimalFactory()
for (t in animalTypes) {
    val c = factory.createAnimal(t)
    println("${c.id} - ${c.name}")
}
```

Output for the preceding code is as follows:

```
1 - Dog
2 - Dog
3 - Cat
4 - Dog
5 - Cat
6 - Cat
```

This was a pretty straightforward example. We provided a common interface for our objects (`Animal`, in this case), then based on some arguments, we decided which concrete class to instantiate.

What if we decided to support different breeds? Take a look at the following code:

```
val animalTypes = listOf("dog" to "bulldog",
                         "dog" to "beagle",
                         "cat" to "persian",
                         "dog" to "poodle",
                         "cat" to "russian blue",
                         "cat" to "siamese")
```

Much like the `downTo` function we saw in `Chapter 1`, *Getting Started with Kotlin*, it looks like an operator, but it's a function that creates a pair of objects: (cat, `siamese`, in our case). We'll come back to it when we discuss the `infix` function in depth.

We can delegate the actual object instantiation to other factories:

```
class AnimalFactory {
    var counter = 0
    private val dogFactory = DogFactory()
    private val catFactory = CatFactory()

    fun createAnimal(animalType: String, animalBreed: String) : Animal {
        return when(animalType.trim().toLowerCase()) {
            "cat" -> catFactory.createDog(animalBreed, ++counter)
            "dog" -> dogFactory.createDog(animalBreed, ++counter)
            else -> throw RuntimeException("Unknown animal $animalType")
        }
    }
}
```

The factory repeats the same pattern again:

```
class DogFactory {
    fun createDog(breed: String, id: Int) =
when(breed.trim().toLowerCase()) {
        "beagle" -> Beagle(id)
        "bulldog" -> Bulldog(id)
        else -> throw RuntimeException("Unknown dog breed $breed")
    }
}
```

You can make sure that you understand this example by implementing `Beagle`, `Bulldog`, `CatFactory`, and all the different breeds of cats by yourself.

The last point to note is how we're now calling our `AnimalFactory` with a pair of arguments:

```
for ((type, breed) in animalTypes) {
    val c = factory.createAnimal(type, breed)
    println(c.name)
}
```

This is called a **destructuring declaration**, and is useful especially when dealing with such pairs of data.

Static Factory Method

The Static Factory Method was popularized by Joshua Bloch in his book *Effective Java*. To understand it better, let's look at the examples from Java standard library itself, the `valueOf()` methods:

```
Long l1 = new Long("1");
Long l2 = Long.valueOf("1");
```

Both the constructor and the `valueOf()` method receive `String` as input and produce `Long` as output.

So, why is the Static Factory Method sometimes better than a constructor?

Advantages of the Static Factory Method

Here are some of the advantages of a Static Factory Method over constructors:

- It provides a better name for the constructor, what it expects, and, sometimes, what it produces.
- We usually don't expect exceptions from a constructor. Exceptions from a regular method, on the other hand, are totally valid.
- Speaking of expectations, we expect the constructor to be fast.

But those are more psychological advantages. There are also some technological advantages to this approach.

Caching

The Static Factory Method may provide caching, as `Long` actually does. Instead of always returning a new instance for any value, `valueOf()` checks in-cache whether this value was already parsed. If it is, it returns a cached instance. Repeatedly calling the Static Factory Method with the same values may produce less garbage for collection than using constructors all the time.

Subclassing

When calling the constructor, we always instantiate the class we specify. On the other hand, calling a Static Factory Method may produce either instance of the class, or one of its subclasses. We'll come to this after discussing the implementation of this design pattern in Kotlin.

Static Factory Method in Kotlin

We've already discussed the `object` keyword earlier in the *Singleton* section. Now we'll see another use of it is a `companion` object.

In Java, Static Factory Methods are declared `static`. But in Kotlin, there's no such keyword. Instead, methods that don't belong to an instance of a class can be declared inside a `companion` object:

```
class NumberMaster {
    companion object {
        fun valueOf(hopefullyNumber: String) : Long {
            return hopefullyNumber.toLong()
        }
    }
}
```

 Companion objects may have a name: companion object Parser, for example. But this is only for clarity of what the goal of this object is.

Calling a `companion` object doesn't require instantiating a class:

```
println(NumberMaster.valueOf("123")) // Prints 123
```

Moreover, calling it on an instance of a class simply won't work, unlike Java:

```
println(NumberMaster().valueOf("123")) // Won't compile
```

 The class may have only one companion object.

Companion object

In Java, Static Factory Methods are declared like this:

```
private static class MyClass {
 // Don't want anybody to use it but me
  private MyClass() {
  }
 // This will replace the public constructor
  public static MyClass create() {
    return new MyClass();
```

```
      }
   }
```

They are called like this:

```
MyClass myClass = MyClass.create();
```

But in Kotlin, there's no such keyword as Static. Instead, methods that don't belong to an instance of a class can be declared inside a companion object.

We discussed the `object` keyword earlier, in the section *Singletons*. Now, we'll look at another use of this important keyword using the following example:

```
class NumberMaster {
    companion object {
        fun valueOf(hopefullyNumber: String) : Long {
            return hopefullyNumber.toLong()
        }
    }
}
```

As you can see, inside our class, we have declared an object that is prefixed by the keyword `companion`.

This object has its own set of functions. What's the benefit of this? You may wonder.

Just like a Java Static method, calling a `companion` object doesn't require the instantiation of a class:

```
println(NumberMaster.valueOf("123")) // Prints 123
```

Moreover, calling it on an instance of a class simply won't work, which is not the case with Java:

```
println(NumberMaster().valueOf("123")) // Won't compile
```

A `companion` object may have a name-Parser, for example. But this is only for clarity of what the goal of this object is.
The class may have only one `companion` object.

By using a `companion` object, we can achieve exactly the same behavior that we see in Java:

```
private class MyClass private constructor() {

    companion object {
        fun create(): MyClass {
```

```
            return MyClass()
        }
    }
}
```

We can now instantiate our object, as shown in the following code:

```
// This won't compile
//val instance = MyClass()

// But this works as it should
val instance = MyClass.create()
```

Kotlin proves itself a very practical language. Every keyword in it has a down-to-earth meaning.

Abstract Factory

Abstract Factory is a greatly misunderstood pattern. It has a notorious reputation for being very complex and bizarre but actually, it's quite simple. If you understood the Factory Method, you'll understand this one in no time. This is because Abstract Factory is a factory of factories. That's all there is to it, really. The factory is a function or class that's able to create other classes. Abstract Factory is a class that creates factories.

You may understand that and still wonder what the usages of such a pattern may be. The main usage of Abstract Factory in the real world would probably be frameworks, most notably Spring Framework, which uses the notion of Abstract Factory to create its components out of annotations and XML files. But since creating our own framework may be quite tiresome, let's take another example where this pattern will be very useful—a strategy game.

We'll call it *CatsCraft 2: Revenge of the Dogs*.

Abstract Factory in action

Our strategy game will consist of buildings and units. Let's start with declaring what all buildings share:

```
interface Building<in UnitType, out ProducedUnit>
        where UnitType : Enum<*>, ProducedUnit : Unit {
    fun build(type: UnitType) : ProducedUnit
}
```

All buildings should implement the `build()` function. Here we see generics in Kotlin for the first time, so let's discuss them a bit.

Introduction to generics in Kotlin

Generics are a way to specify the relationships between types. Well, that didn't help explain much, did it? Let's try again. Generics are an abstraction of types. Nope, still awful.

We'll try an example, then:

```
val listOfStrings = mutableListOf("a", "b", "c")
```

Ok, that's easy; we've covered it a lot of times. This code simply creates a list of strings. But what does it actually mean?

Let's try the following line of code:

```
listOfStrings.add(1)
```

This line doesn't compile. That's because the `mutableListOf()` function uses generics:

```
public fun <T> mutableListOf(vararg elements: T): MutableList<T>
```

Generics create an expectation. No matter which type we use to create our list, from now on we can only put that type in it. It's a great language feature because, on the one hand, we can generalize our data structures or algorithms. No matter what types they hold, they'll still work in exactly the same way.

On the other hand, we still have type safety. The `listOfStrings.first()` function is guaranteed to return a `String` (in this case) and nothing else.

In terms of generics, Kotlin uses an approach that is similar to, but slightly different from, Java. We won't cover all the aspects of generics in this section, but will only provide some guidance to better understand this example. As we go on, we'll encounter more uses of generics.

Let's look at another example.

We'll create a class called `Box`. Boring, I know:

```
class Box<T> {
    private var inside: T? = null

    fun put(t: T) {
```

```
        inside = t
    }
    fun get(): T? = inside
}
```

What's great about this box, though, is that by using generics, I can put just about anything in it, for example, a cat:

```
class Cat
```

When I create an instance of a box, I specify what it can hold:

```
val box = Box<Cat>()
```

At compile time, the generics will make sure that it will only hold objects of the correct type:

```
box.put(Cat()) // This will work
val cat = box.get() // This will always return a Cat, because that's what
our box holds
box.put("Cat") // This won't work, String is not a Cat
```

As you may know, Java uses the wildcards ? extends, and super keywords to specify read-only and write-only types.

Kotlin uses the concepts of in, out, and where.

A type that is marked as in can be used as a parameter but not as a return value. This is also called covariance. In fact, it means that we can return ProducedUnit or something that inherits from it, but not something that is above ProducedUnit in the hierarchy.

Types that are marked as out can be used only as a return value, not as a parameter. This is called contravariance.

Furthermore, we may introduce constraints on types using the where keyword. In our case, we require that the first type implements the Type interface, while the second type implements the Unit interface.

The names of the types themselves, UnitType and ProducedUnit, could be anything we want, T and P, for example. But for the sake of clarity, we'll use more verbose names.

Back to our bases

HQ is a special building that can produce other buildings. It keeps track of all the buildings it had built up until now. The same type of building can be built more than once:

```
class HQ {
    val buildings = mutableListOf<Building<*, Unit>>()

    fun buildBarracks(): Barracks {
        val b = Barracks()
        buildings.add(b)
        return b
    }

    fun buildVehicleFactory(): VehicleFactory {
        val vf = VehicleFactory()
        buildings.add(vf)
        return vf
    }
}
```

 You may be wondering what the star (*) means as regards generics. It's called a star projection, and it means *I don't know anything about this type.* It's similar to Java's raw types, but it's type safe.

All other buildings produce units. Units can be either infantry or armored vehicle:

```
interface Unit

interface Vehicle : Unit

interface Infantry : Unit
```

Infantry can be either riflemen or rocket soldier:

```
class Rifleman : Infantry

class RocketSoldier : Infantry

enum class InfantryUnits {
    RIFLEMEN,
    ROCKET_SOLDIER
}
```

Here we see the `enum` keyword for the first time. Vehicles are either tanks or **armored personnel carriers (APCs)**:

```
class APC : Vehicle

class Tank : Vehicle

enum class VehicleUnits {
    APC,
    TANK
}
```

A barracks is a building that produces infantry:

```
class Barracks : Building<InfantryUnits, Infantry> {
    override fun build(type: InfantryUnits): Infantry {
        return when (type) {
            RIFLEMEN -> Rifleman()
            ROCKET_SOLDIER -> RocketSoldier()
        }
    }
}
```

We don't need the `else` block in our `when`. That's because we use `enum`, and Kotlin makes sure that `when` on `enum` is exhaustive.

A vehicle factory is a building that produces different types of armored vehicles:

```
class VehicleFactory : Building<VehicleUnits, Vehicle> {
    override fun build(type: VehicleUnits) = when (type) {
        APC -> APC()
        TANK -> Tank()
    }
}
```

We can make sure that we can build different units now:

```
val hq = HQ()
val barracks1 = hq.buildBarracks()
val barracks2 = hq.buildBarracks()
val vehicleFactory1 = hq.buildVehicleFactory()
```

And now on to producing units:

```
val units = listOf(
        barracks1.build(InfantryUnits.RIFLEMEN),
        barracks2.build(InfantryUnits.ROCKET_SOLDIER),
        barracks2.build(InfantryUnits.ROCKET_SOLDIER),
        vehicleFactory1.build(VehicleUnits.TANK),
        vehicleFactory1.build(VehicleUnits.APC),
        vehicleFactory1.build(VehicleUnits.APC)
)
```

We've already seen the `listOf()` function from the standard library. It will create a read-only list of different units that our buildings produce. You can iterate over this list and make sure that those are indeed the units we require.

Making improvements

One may claim that having the `VehicleFactory` and `Barracks` classes is too cumbersome. They don't have any state, after all. Instead, we can replace them with objects.

Instead of the previous implementation of `buildBarracks()`, we can have the following:

```
fun buildBarracks(): Building<InfantryUnits, Infantry> {
    val b = object : Building<InfantryUnits, Infantry> {
        override fun build(type: InfantryUnits): Infantry {
            return when (type) {
                InfantryUnits.RIFLEMEN -> Rifleman()
                InfantryUnits.ROCKET_SOLDIER -> RocketSoldier()
            }
        }
    }
    buildings.add(b)
    return b
}
```

We've already seen two different usages of the `object` keyword: once in the Singleton design pattern, and another time in the Factory Method design pattern. Here is the third way we can use it: for creating anonymous classes on the fly. After all, `Barracks` is a building that, given `InfantryUnitType`, produces `Infantry`.

If our logic is straightforward, we can even shorten the declaration a bit more:

```
fun buildVehicleFactory(): Building<VehicleUnits, Vehicle> {
    val vf = object : Building<VehicleUnits, Vehicle> {
        override fun build(type: VehicleUnits) = when (type) {
```

```
            VehicleUnits.APC -> APC()
            VehicleUnits.TANK -> Tank()
        }
    }
    buildings.add(vf)

    return vf
}
```

Let's go to the beginning of this chapter. We said that Abstract Factory combines a number of related factories. So, what's common to all factories in our case? They're all buildings and they all produce units.

Having that principle in mind, you could apply it to many different cases. If you're familiar with strategy games, usually they have at least two different factions. Each may have different structures and units. To achieve that, you can repeat this pattern as many times as needed.

Let's assume we have two different factions now, cats and dogs, and Tanks and Rocket Infantry are only prerogatives of this faction. Dogs have Heavy Tanks and Grenadiers instead. What changes do we need to make in our system?

First, HQ becomes an interface:

```
interface HQ {
    fun buildBarracks(): Building<InfantryUnits, Infantry>
    fun buildVehicleFactory(): Building<VehicleUnits, Vehicle>
}
```

What was HQ previously now becomes CatHQ:

```
class CatHQ : HQ {
// Remember to add override to your methods
}
```

And DogHQ will have to repeat the same steps, but with a different construction logic.

This ability to accommodate big changes is what makes Abstract Factory so powerful in some use cases.

Builder

Sometimes, our objects are very simple, and have only one constructor, be it an empty or non-empty one. But sometimes, their creation is very complex, and based on a lot of parameters. We've seen one pattern already that provides *a better constructor*—the Static Factory Method design pattern. Now, we'll discuss Builder design pattern, which is somewhat similar and somewhat different.

Composing an email

As a software architect, one of my main channels of communication is email. Probably this is true of most software development roles.

An email has the following:

- An address (at least one is mandatory)
- CC (zero or more, optional)
- Title (optional)
- Body (optional)
- Attachment (zero or more, optional)

Let's assume I'm really lazy, and would like to schedule emails to be sent while I'm actually biking around the neighborhood.

The actual scheduling logic will be postponed to Chapter 8, *Threads and Coroutines*, and Chapter 9, *Designed for Concurrency*, which discuss scheduling and concurrency. For now, let's see what our `Mail` class may look like:

```
data class Mail(val to: String,
                val cc: List<String>,
                val bcc: List<String>,
                val title: String?,
                val message: String)
```

So, we've already seen `data class` in action in the previous chapters. We've also discussed nullable and non-nullable types, such as `String?` versus `String`.

Now is a good time to discuss how collections work in Kotlin, since this is the first time we have a class that deals with them directly.

Collection types in Kotlin

One of the main Kotlin goals is Java interoperability. So it's no wonder that Kotlin collections are interoperable with Java. When you specify that your functions receives `List<T>`, it is actually the same Java `List<T>` you're familiar with.

But Kotlin differentiates between mutable and immutable collections. The `listOf()` function is delegated to `Arrays.asList()`, and produces an immutable list, while `mutableListOf()` simply calls `ArrayList()`.

On top of data, Kotlin collection has many useful extension methods, which we'll discuss later.

Creating an email – first attempt

So, at 10 A.M., I plan to drink a coffee in my local cafe. But I also want to contact my manager, since my payslip didn't arrive yesterday. I attempt to create my first email like so:

```
val mail = Mail("manager@company.com", // TO
    null,    // CC
    null,    // BCC
    "Ping", // Title
    null    // Message)
```

This may have worked in Java, but in Kotlin this wouldn't compile, since we cannot pass `null` to `List<String>`. Null-safety is very important in Kotlin:

```
val mail = Mail("manager@company.com", // TO
    listOf(),   // CC
    listOf(),   // BCC
    "Ping",     // Title
    null        // Message)
```

Note that since our constructor receives a lot of arguments, I had to put in some comments, so I wouldn't get lost.

The Kotlin compiler is smart enough to infer the type of list that we pass. Since our constructor receives `List<String>`, it's enough to pass `listOf()` for an empty list. We don't need to specify the type like so: `listOf<String>()`. In Java, Diamond Operator serves the same purpose.

Oh, but I forgot about attachments. Let's change our constructor:

```
data class Mail(val to: String,
            val cc: List<String>,
            val bcc: List<String>,
            val title: String?,
            val message: String?,
            val attachments: List<java.io.File>)
```

But then our instantiation stops compiling again:

```
val mail = Mail("manager@company.com", // TO
    listOf(), listOf(),
    "Ping",
    null) // Compilation error, No value passed for for parameter
'attachments'
```

This clearly becomes a mess.

Creating an email – second attempt

Let's try a fluent setter approach instead. We'll have only mandatory fields in our constructor, and all others will become setters, so the creation of a new email would look something like this:

```
Mail("manager@company.com").title("Ping").cc(listOf<String>())
```

That's a lot nicer for many reasons:

- The order of fields can now be arbitrary, unlike with the constructor.
- It's clearer which field is being set, no need for comments anymore.
- Optional fields don't need to be set at all. As an example, the CC field is set, while the BCC field is omitted.

Let's see one way of implementing this approach. There are other convenient ways to do it, which we'll discuss in Chapter 10, *Idioms and Anti-Patterns*:

```
data class Mail(// Stays the same
                private var _message: String = "",
                // ...) {
    fun message(message: String) : Mail {
        _message = message
        return this
    }
}
```

```
    // Pattern repeats for every other variable
}
```

 Using underscores for private variables is a common convention in Kotlin. It allows us to avoid repeating `this.message = message` and mistakes such as `message = message`.

This is nice, and very similar to what we may achieve in Java. Although we did have to make our message mutable now. But Kotlin provides two other ways that you may find even more useful.

Creating an email – the Kotlin way

Like some other modern languages, Kotlin provides us with the ability to set *default values* for function parameters:

```
data class Mail(val to: String,
    val title: String = "",
    val message: String = "",
    val cc: List<String> = listOf(),
    val bcc: List<String> = listOf(),
    val attachments: List<java.io.File> = listOf())
```

So, if you would like to send an email without CC, you can do it like that now:

```
val mail = Mail("one@recepient.org", "Hi", "How are you")
```

But what about the case where you want to send an email with BCC? Also, not having to specify order with fluent setters was very handy. Kotlin has *named arguments* for that:

```
val mail = Mail(title= "Hello", message="There", to="my@dear.cat")
```

Combining default parameters with named arguments makes creating complex objects in Kotlin a lot easier than before. There's another way to achieve somewhat similar behavior: the `apply()` function. This is one of the extension functions that every object in Kotlin has. In order to use this approach, though, we'll need to make all the optional fields variables instead of values:

Then we can create our email like this:

```
val mail = Mail("hello@mail.com").apply {
    message = "Something"
    title = "Apply"
}
```

The `apply()` function is the only one out of the family of **scoping functions**. We'll discuss how scoping functions work and are their uses in later chapters. Now, while my boss thinks I'm working hard sending all these emails, I can go back to my coffee. It's getting cold now!

Creating an email – the Kotlin way – second attempt

Let's try a fluent setter approach, instead. We'll have only mandatory fields in our constructor, and all of the others will become setters. So to create a new email, we no longer need to do the following:

```
val mail = Mail("manager@company.com")
mail.title("Ping")
mail.cc(listOf<String>())
```

Instead, we will do the following:

```
Mail("manager@company.com").title("Ping").cc(listOf<String>())
```

Fluent setters allow us to chain one set call to another.

That's a lot nicer for a couple of reasons:

- The order of fields can now be arbitrary, unlike the order used with the constructor.
- It's clearer which field is being set; no more need for comments.
- Optional fields don't need to be set at all. As an example, the **CC** field is set while the **BCC** field is omitted.

Let's look at one way of implementing this approach. There are other convenient ways to do this, which we'll discuss in Chapter 10, *Idioms and Anti-Patterns*:

```
data class Mail(// Stays the same
                private var _message: String = "",
                // ...) {
    fun message(message: String) : Mail {
        _message = message
return this }
    // Pattern repeats for every other variable
  }
```

Using underscores for private variables is a common convention in Kotlin. It allows us to avoid repeating the phrase `this.message = message` and mistakes, such as `message = message`.

This is nice and is very similar to what we may achieve in Java, although we did have to make our message mutable.

We can also implement a full-blown builder design pattern, of course:

```
class MailBuilder(val to: String) {
    private var mail: Mail = Mail(to)
    fun title(title: String): MailBuilder {
        mail.title = title
        return this
    }
    // Repeated for other properties
    fun build(): Mail {
        return mail
    }
}
```

You can use it to create your email in the following way:

```
val email = MailBuilder("hello@hello.com").title("What's up?").build()
```

But Kotlin provides two other ways that you may find even more useful.

Prototype

This design pattern is all about customization and creating objects that are similar but slightly different. To understand it better, we'll start with an example.

Building your own PC

Imagine that you have a shop where you sell PCs.

Regular PC consists of the foll:

- Motherboard
- CPU
- Graphical card
- RAM

Most of your customers don't actually care what components you put in this PC. What they do care about is whether this PC will be able to run *Magnificent Pilfering Car 7* at 60fps (which is frame per second).

So, you decide to build it like that:

```
data class PC(val motherboard: String = "Terasus XZ27",
              val cpu: String = "Until Atom K500",
              val ram: String = "8GB Microcend BBR5",
              val graphicCard: String = "nKCF 8100TZ")
```

So when a new customer comes in wanting to try out this game everybody is talking about in the neighborhood, you just do:

```
val pc = PC()
```

And they are already off toward home, ready to share their newest experiences from MPC7. Actually, your business goes so well that you have one PC just sitting there, ready for the next customer to come in.

But then another customer arrives. And this one is tech savvy. So, frankly, they think that for the games they play, a *nKCF 8100TZ graphic card* wouldn't be enough at all. They've also read that there's now *BBR6 RAM* available and they want *16 GB* of it. And of course, they want it right away. But they're willing to pay in cash.

That's the moment you wish that you could just modify this PC that's sitting in your warehouse a little, instead of assembling a new one.

Starting from a prototype

The whole idea of a prototype is to be able to clone an object easily. There are a number of reasons you may want to do this:

- Creating your object is very expensive. You need to fetch it from the database.
- You create objects that are similar but different from one another, and you don't want to repeat similar parts over and over again.

 There are also more advanced reasons to use this pattern. JavaScript language, for example, uses prototypes to implement inheritance-like behavior without having classes.

Luckily, Kotlin fixes the *broken* Java `clone()` method. For data classes, there's the `copy()` method, which takes an existing data class, and creates a new copy of it, optionally changing some of its attributes in the process:

```
val pcFromWarehouse = PC() // Our boring PC

val pwnerPC = pcFromWarehouse.copy(graphicCard = "nKCF 8999ZTXX",
        ram = "16GB BBR6") // Amazing PC

println(pwnerPC) // Make sure that PC created correctly
```

By default, the `clone()` method creates a shallow copy, which may be unexpected for less experienced developers. It's very hard to implement the `clone()` method correctly in Java. You can read about the various pitfalls at `https://dzone.com/articles/shallow-and-deep-java-cloning`.

Similar to what we've seen in the Builder design pattern, named arguments allow us to specify attributes that we can change in any order.

The only thing that's left is for you to count the cash and buy some more of those *nKCF graphic cards*. Just in case.

Summary

In this chapter, we learned when and how to use design patterns from the Creational family. We learned about different usages of the `object` keyword: as Singleton, as a container for the Static Factory Methods, and as an anonymous implementation of an interface. We then saw the workings of the destructuring declaration and generics in Kotlin with the use of the `in`, `out`, and `where` keywords. We also learned about the default parameter values and named arguments, followed by the `copy()` function for data classes.

In the next chapter, we'll cover the second family of design patterns, Structural patterns. Those patterns help extend the functionality of our objects.

3
Understanding Structural Patterns

This chapter covers structural patterns in Kotlin. In general, structural patterns deal with relationships between objects.

We'll discuss how to extend the functionality of our objects without producing complex class hierarchies and how to adapt to changes in the future or how to fix some of the decisions taken in the past, as well as how to reduce the memory footprint of our program.

In this chapter, we will cover the following topics:

- Decorator
- Adapter
- Bridge
- Composite
- Facade
- Flyweight
- Proxy

Decorator

In the previous chapter, we discussed the **Prototype** design pattern, which allowed for creating instances of classes with slightly (or not so slightly) different data.

What if we would like to create a set of classes with slightly different behavior though? Well, since functions in Kotlin are first-class citizens (more on that in a bit), you could use the Prototype design pattern to achieve that. After all, that's what JavaScript does successfully. But the goal of this chapter is to discuss another approach to the same problem. After all, design patterns are all about approaches.

By implementing this design pattern, we allow the user of our code to specify which abilities he or she wants to add.

Enhancing a class

Your boss—sorry, scrum master—came to you yesterday with an urgent requirement. From now on, all map data structures in your system are to become HappyMaps.

What, you don't know what HappyMaps are? They are the hottest stuff going around right now. They are just like the regular HashMap, but when you override an existing value, they print the following output:

Yay! Very useful

So, what you do is type the following code in your editor:

```
class HappyMap<K, V>: HashMap<K, V>() {
    override fun put(key: K, value: V): V? {
        return super.put(key, value).apply {
            this?.let {
                println("Yay! $key")
            }
        }
    }
}
```

We've seen apply() already when we discussed the **Builder** design pattern in the previous chapter and this?.let { ... } is a nicer way of saying if (this != null) { ... }.

We can test our solution using the following code:

```
fun main(args : Array<String>) {
    val happy = HappyMap<String, String>()
    happy["one"] = "one"
    happy["two"] = "two"
    happy["two"] = "three"
}
```

The preceding code prints the following output as expected:

Yay! two

That was the only overridden key.

Operator overloading

Hold on a second, how do square brackets keep working when we extended a map? Aren't they some kind of magic?

Well, actually no. No magic there. As you may have guessed by the title of this section, Kotlin supports operator overloading. Operator overloading means that the same operator acts differently, depending on the type of arguments it receives.

If you've ever worked with Java, you're familiar with operator overloading already. Think of how the plus operator works. Let take a look at the example given here:

```
System.out.println(1 + 1); // 2
System.out.println("1" + "1") // 11
```

Based on whether two arguments are either strings or integers, the + sign acts differently.

But, in the Java world, this is something that only the language itself is allowed to do. The following code won't compile, no matter how hard we try:

```
List<String> a = Arrays.asList("a");
List<String> b = Collections.singletonList("b"); // Same for one argument
List<String> c = a + b;
```

 In Java 9, there's also `List.of()`, which serves a similar purpose to `Arrays.asList()`.

In Kotlin, the same code prints `[a, b]`:

```
val a = listOf("a")
val b = listOf("b")
println(a + b)
```

Well, that makes a lot of sense, but maybe it's just a language feature:

```
data class Json(val j: String)
val j1 = Json("""{"a": "b"}""")
val j2 = Json("""{"c": "d"}""")
println(j1 + j2) // Compilation error!
```

Told you it was magic! You cannot simply join two arbitrary classes together.

But wait. What if we create an extension function for our `Json` class, `plus()`, as follows:

```
operator fun Json.plus(j2: Json): Json {
    // Code comes here
}
```

Everything but the first keyword, `operator`, should look familiar to you. We extend the `Json` object with a new function that gets another `Json` and returns `Json`.

We implement the function body like this:

```
val jsonFields = this.j.split(":") + j2.j.split(":")
val s = (jsonFields).joinToString(":")
return Json ("""{$s}""")
```

This isn't really joining any JSON, but it joins `Json` in our example. We take values from our `Json`, values from the other `Json`, then join them together and put some curly brackets around them.

Now look at this line:

```
println(j1 + j2)
```

The preceding code prints the following output:

```
{{"a": "b"}:{"c": "d"}}
```

Actually, it will print: `Json(j={{"a": "b"}:{"c": "d"}})`. This is because we didn't override the `toString()` method in our example for brevity.

So, what's this `operator` keyword about?

Unlike some other languages, you cannot override every operator that exists in Kotlin languages, just a chosen few.

 Albeit limited, the list of all operators that can be overridden is quite long, so we'll not list it here. You can refer to it in the official documentation: `https://kotlinlang.org/docs/reference/operator-overloading.html`.

Try renaming your extension method to:

- `prus()`: Just a name with a typo
- `minus()`: The existing function that correlates with the – sign

You will see that your code stops compiling.

The square brackets that we started with are called **indexed access operators** and correlate to the `get(x)` and `set(x, y)` methods.

Dude, where's my map?

The next day, your product manager reaches out to you. Apparently, they want a `SadMap` now, which gets *sad* each time a key is removed from it. Following the previous pattern, you extend the map again:

```
class SadMap<K, V>: HashMap<K, V>() {
    override fun remove(key: K): V? {
        println("Okay...")
        return super.remove(key)
    }
}
```

But then the chief architect asks that in some cases, a map would be happy and sad at the same time. The CTO already has a great idea for a `SuperSadMap` that will print the following output twice:

Okay...

So, what we need is the ability to combine the behaviors of our objects.

The great combinator

We'll start a bit differently this time. Instead of composing our solution piece by piece, we'll look at the complete solution and decompose it. The code here will help you understand why:

```
class HappyMap<K, V>(private val map: MutableMap<K, V> =
mutableMapOf()) :
    MutableMap<K, V> by map {

    override fun put(key: K, value: V): V? {
        return map.put(key, value).apply {
            this?.let { println("Yay! $key") }
        }
    }
}
```

The hardest part here is to understand the signature. What we need in the Decorator pattern is:

- To be able to receive the object we're decorating
- To keep a reference to it
- When our Decorator is called, we decide if we would like to change the behavior of the object we're holding, or to delegate the call

Since we need to actually do a lot of stuff, this declaration is quite complex. After all, it does a lot of stuff in one line, which should be quite impressive. Let's break it down line by line:

```
class HappyMap<K, V>(...
```

Our class is named `HappyMap` and has two type arguments, `K` and `V`, which stand for **key** and **value**:

```
... (private val map: MutableMap<K, V> ...
```

In our constructor, we receive `MutableMap`, with types `K` and `V`, the same as ours:

```
... = mutableMapOf()) ...
```

If no map was passed, we initialize our property with the default argument value, which is an empty mutable map:

```
... : MutableMap<K, V> ...
```

Our class extends the `MutableMap` interface:

```
... by map
```

It also **delegates** all methods that weren't overridden to the object that we will wrap, in our case a map.

 The code for `SadMap` using delegate is omitted, but you can easily reproduce it by combining the declaration of `HappyMap` and the previous implementation of `SadMap`.

Let's compose our `SadHappyMap` now, to please the chief architect:

```
val sadHappy = SadMap(HappyMap<String, String>())
sadHappy["one"] = "one"
sadHappy["two"] = "two"
```

```
sadHappy["two"] = "three"
sadHappy["a"] = "b"
sadHappy.remove("a")
```

We get the following output:

```
Yay! two // Because it delegates to HappyMap
Okay...  // Because it is a SadMap
```

In the same way, we can now create `SuperSadMap`:

```
val superSad = SadMap(HappyMap<String, String>())
```

And we can please the CTO too.

 The Decorator design pattern is widely used in the `java.io.*` package, with classes such as reader and writer.

Caveats

The Decorator design pattern is great because it lets us compose objects *on the fly*. Using Kotlin's `by` keyword will make it simple to implement. But there are still limitations that you need to take care of.

First, you cannot see *inside* of the Decorator:

```
println(sadHappy is SadMap<*, *>) // True
```

That's the top wrapper, so no problem there:

```
println(sadHappy is MutableMap<*, *>) // True
```

That's the interface we implement, so the compiler knows about it:

```
println(sadHappy is HappyMap<*, *>) // False
```

Although `SadMap` contains `HappyMap` and may behave like it, it is not a `HappyMap`! Keep that in mind while performing casts and type checks.

Second, which is related to the first point, is the fact that since Decorator is usually not aware directly of which class it wraps, it's hard to do optimizations. Imagine that our CTO requested `SuperSadMap` to print `Okay... Okay...` and that's it, on the same line. For that, we would need to either capture the entire output, or investigate all the classes that we will wrap, which are quite complex tasks.

Keep these points in mind when you use this powerful design pattern. It allows for adding new responsibilities to an object dynamically (in our case, printing `Yay` is a responsibility), instead of subclassing the object. Each new responsibility is a new wrapping layer you add.

Adapter

The main goal of an Adapter, or Wrapper, as it's sometimes called, is to convert one interface to another interface. In the physical world, the best example would be an electrical plug Adapter, or a USB Adapter.

Imagine yourself in a hotel room in the late evening, with 7% battery left on your phone. Your phone charger was left in the office, at the other end of the city. You only have an EU plug charger with a USB mini cable. But your phone is USB type-C, because you had to upgrade. And you're in New York, so all of your outlets are of course US type-A. What do you do? Oh, it's easy. You look for a USB mini to USB Type-C Adapter in the middle of the night and hope you also don't forget to bring that EU to US plug Adapter while you're at it. Only 5% battery left. Time is running out.

So, now that we understand a bit better what adapters are for in the physical world, let's see how we can apply the same in code.

Let's start with interfaces:

```
interface UsbTypeC
interface UsbMini

interface EUPlug
interface USPlug
```

Now we can declare a phone and a power outlet:

```
// Power outlet exposes USPlug interface
fun powerOutlet() : USPlug {
    return object : USPlug {}
}
```

```
fun cellPhone(chargeCable: UsbTypeC) {

}
```

Our charger is wrong in every way, of course:

```
// Charger accepts EUPlug interface and exposes UsbMini interface
fun charger(plug: EUPlug) : UsbMini {
    return object : UsbMini {}
}
```

Here we get the following errors:

```
Type mismatch: required EUPlug, found USPlug: charger(powerOutlet())

Type mismatch: required UsbTypeC, found UsbMini:
cellPhone(charger(powerOutlet()))
```

Different adapters

So, we need two types of adapters.

In Java, you would usually create a pair of classes for that purpose. In Kotlin, we can replace those with extension functions.

We could adopt the US plug to work with the EU plug by using the following extension function:

```
fun USPlug.toEUPlug() : EUPlug {
    return object : EUPlug {
        // Do something to convert
    }
}
```

We can create a USB Adapter between mini USB and type-C USB in a similar way:

```
fun UsbMini.toUsbTypeC() : UsbTypeC {
    return object : UsbTypeC {
        // Do something to convert
    }
}
```

And finally, we get back online by combining all those adapters together:

```
cellPhone(
    charger(
        powerOutlet().toEUPlug()
    ).toUsbTypeC()
)
```

As you can see, we don't need to compose one object inside the other to adapt them. Nor, luckily, do we need to inherit both interface and implementation. With Kotlin, our code stays short and to the point.

Adapters in the real world

You've probably encountered those adapters too. Mostly, they adapt between *concepts* and *implementations*. For example, let's take the concept of *collection* versus the concept of a *stream*:

```
val l = listOf("a", "b", "c")

fun <T> streamProcessing(stream: Stream<T>) {
    // Do something with stream
}
```

You cannot simply pass a collection to a function that receives a stream, even though it may make sense:

```
streamProcessing(l) // Doesn't compile
```

Luckily, collections provide us with the .stream() method:

```
streamProcessing(l.stream()) // Adapted successfully
```

Caveats of using adapters

Did you ever plug a 110v US appliance into a 220v EU socket through an Adapter, and fry it totally?

That's something that may also happen to your code, if you're not careful. The following example, which uses another Adapter, compiles well:

```
fun <T> collectionProcessing(c: Collection<T>) {
    for (e in c) {
        println(e)
```

```
        }
    }

    val s = Stream.generate { 42 }
    collectionProcessing(s.toList())
```

But it never completes, because `Stream.generate()` produces an infinite list of integers. So, be careful, and adapt this pattern wisely.

Bridge

Unlike some other design patterns we've met, Bridge is less about a smart way to compose objects, and more about guidelines on how not to abuse inheritance. The way it works is actually very simple.

Let's go back to the strategy game we're building. We have an interface for all our infantry units:

```
interface Infantry {
    fun move(x: Long, y: Long)

    fun attack(x: Long, y: Long)
}
```

We have the concrete implementations:

```
open class Rifleman : Infantry {
    override fun attack(x: Long, y: Long) {
        // Shoot
    }

    override fun move(x: Long, y: Long) {
        // Move at its own pace
    }
}

open class Grenadier : Infantry {
    override fun attack(x: Long, y: Long) {
        // Throw grenades
    }

    override fun move(x: Long, y: Long) {
        // Moves slowly, grenades are heavy
    }
}
```

What if we want to have the ability to upgrade our units?

Upgraded units should have twice the damage, but move at the same pace:

```
class UpgradedRifleman : Rifleman() {
    override fun attack(x: Long, y: Long) {
        // Shoot twice as much
    }
}

class UpgradedGrenadier : Grenadier() {
    override fun attack(x: Long, y: Long) {
        // Throw pack of grenades
    }
}
```

Now, our game designer has decided that we also need a light version of those units. That is, they attack in the same way as regular units, but move at twice the speed:

```
class LightRifleman : Rifleman() {
    override fun move(x: Long, y: Long) {
        // Running with rifle
    }
}

class LightGrenadier : Grenadier() {
    override fun move(x: Long, y: Long) {
        // I've been to gym, pack of grenades is no problem
    }
}
```

Since design patterns are all about adapting to change, here comes our dear designer, and asks that all infantry units be able to shout, that is, to proclaim their unit name loud and clear:

```
interface Infantry {
    // As before, move() and attack() functions

    fun shout() // Here comes the change
}
```

What are we to do now?

We go and change the implementation of six different classes, feeling lucky that there are only six and not sixteen.

Bridging changes

Depending on the way you look at it, the **Bridge** design pattern may resemble Adapter, which we already discussed, or **Strategy**, which we'll discuss in the next chapter.

The idea behind the Bridge design pattern is to flatten the class hierarchy, which is currently three levels deep:

```
Infantry --> Rifleman  --> Upgraded Rifleman
--> Light Rifleman
        --> Grenadier --> Upgraded Grenadier
                      --> Light Grenadier
```

Why do we have this complex hierarchy?

It's because we have three orthogonal properties: weapon type, weapon strength, and movement speed.

Say instead, we were to pass those properties to the constructor of a class that implements the same interface we were using all along:

```
class Soldier(private val weapon: Weapon,
              private val legs: Legs) : Infantry {
    override fun attack(x: Long, y: Long) {
        // Find target
        // Shoot
        weapon.causeDamage()
    }

    override fun move(x: Long, y: Long) {
        // Compute direction
        // Move at its own pace
        legs.move()
    }
}
```

The properties that `Soldier` receives should be interfaces, so we could choose their implementation later:

```
interface Weapon {
    fun causeDamage(): PointsOfDamage
}

interface Legs {
    fun move(): Meters
}
```

But what are `Meters` and `PointsOfDamage`? Are those classes or interfaces we declared somewhere?

Let's take a short detour.

Type aliases

First, we'll look at how they're declared:

```
typealias PointsOfDamage = Long
typealias Meters = Int
```

We use a new keyword here, `typealias`. From now on, we can use `Meters` instead of plain old `Int` to return from our `move()` method. They aren't new types. The Kotlin compiler will always translate `PointsOfDamage` to `Long` during compilation. Using them provides two advantages:

- Better semantics, as in our case. We can tell exactly what the meaning of the value we're returning is.
- One of the main goals of Kotlin is to be concise. Type aliases allow us to hide complex generic expressions. We'll expand on this in the following sections.

You're in the army now

Back to our `Soldier` class. We want it to be as adaptable as possible, right? He knows he can move or use his weapon for greater good. But how exactly is he going to do that?

We totally forgot to implement those parts! Let's start with our weapons:

```
class Grenade : Weapon {
    override fun causeDamage() = GRENADE_DAMAGE
}

class GrenadePack : Weapon {
    override fun causeDamage() = GRENADE_DAMAGE * 3
}

class Rifle : Weapon {
    override fun causeDamage() = RIFLE_DAMAGE
}
```

```
class MachineGun : Weapon {
    override fun causeDamage() = RIFLE_DAMAGE * 2
}
```

Now, let's look at how we can move:

```
class RegularLegs : Legs {
    override fun move() = REGULAR_SPEED
}

class AthleticLegs : Legs {
    override fun move() = REGULAR_SPEED * 2
}
```

Constants

We define all parameters as constants:

```
const val GRENADE_DAMAGE : PointsOfDamage = 5L
const val RIFLE_DAMAGE = 3L
const val REGULAR_SPEED : Meters = 1
```

Those values are very effective, since they are known during compilation.

Unlike `static final` variables in Java, they cannot be placed inside a class. You should place them either at the top level of your package or nest them inside `object`.

 Note that although Kotlin has type inference, we can specify the types of our constants explicitly, and even use type aliases. How about having `DEFAULT_TIMEOUT : Seconds = 60` instead of `DEFAULT_TIMEOUT_SECONDS = 60` in your code?

A lethal weapon

What is left for us is to see that with the new hierarchy, we can still do the exact same things:

```
val rifleman = Soldier(Rifle(), RegularLegs())
val grenadier = Soldier(Grenade(), RegularLegs())
val upgradedGrenadier = Soldier(GrenadePack(), RegularLegs())
val upgradedRifleman = Soldier(MachineGun(), RegularLegs())
val lightRifleman = Soldier(Rifle(), AthleticLegs())
val lightGrenadier = Soldier(Grenade(), AthleticLegs())
```

Now, our hierarchy looks like this:

```
Infantry --> Soldier

Weapon --> Rifle
       --> MachineGun
       --> Grenade
       --> GrenadePack

Legs --> RegularLegs
     --> AthleticLegs
```

Much simpler to extend and also to comprehend. Unlike some other design patterns we discussed before, we didn't use any special language feature we didn't know about, just some engineering best practices.

Composite

You may finish this section with a lingering feeling that this pattern is a bit awkward. That's because it has a soul mate, it's accompanying pattern, **Iterator**, which we'll discuss in the next chapter. When both are combined, that's where they really shine. So, if you're feeling confused, come back to this pattern after you have got acquainted with **Iterator** too.

Having said that, we can start analyzing this pattern. It may look a bit strange to have a **Composite** design pattern. After all, aren't all **Structural Patterns** about composing objects?

Much like in the case of the Bridge design pattern, the name may not reflect its true benefits.

Get together

Going back to our strategy game, we have a new concept: a squad. A squad consists of zero or more infantry units. This would be a good example of a somewhat complex data structure.

Here are the interfaces and classes we have:

```
interface InfantryUnit

class Rifleman : InfantryUnit
```

```
class Sniper : InfantryUnit
```

How would you implement that? We'll see it in the next section.

The Squad

Squad, clearly, must be a collection of infantry units. So, it should be easy:

```
class Squad(val infantryUnits: MutableList<InfantryUnit> =
mutableListOf())
```

We even set up a default parameter value, so the other programmer won't need to pass his own list of soldiers unless he really needs too. MutableList suits us well here, since we may add units later.

To make sure it works, we'll create three soldiers and put them inside:

```
val miller = Rifleman()
val caparzo = Rifleman()
val jackson = Sniper()

val squad = Squad()

squad.infantryUnits.add(miller)
squad.infantryUnits.add(caparzo)
squad.infantryUnits.add(jackson)

println(squad.infantryUnits.size) // Prints 3
```

But the next day, Dave, that's the other programmer, comes to us with a new requirement. He thinks it consists of too many lines of code to add soldiers one by one, or even to use mutableListOf() to pass them.

He would like to initialize squads like this:

```
val squad = Squad(miller, caparzo, jackson)
```

That looks nice, but how in the name of all the squads are we going to do that?

Varargs and secondary constructors

Up until now, we were always using the primary constructor of the class. That's the one declared after the class name. But in Java, we can define more than one constructor for a class. Why does Kotlin limit us to only one?

Actually, it doesn't. We can define secondary constructors for a class using the `constructor` keyword:

```
class Squad(val infantryUnits: MutableList<InfantryUnit> = mutableListOf())
{
    constructor(first: InfantryUnit) : this(mutableListOf()) {
        this.infantryUnits.add(first)
    }

    constructor(first: InfantryUnit,
                second: InfantryUnit) : this(first) {
        this.infantryUnits.add(second)
    }

    constructor(first: InfantryUnit,
                second: InfantryUnit,
                third: InfantryUnit) :
        this(first, second) {
        this.infantryUnits.add(third)
    }
}
```

Note how we delegate one constructor to another:

```
    constructor(first: InfantryUnit) : this(mutableListOf()) {
    }                                          ⇑
                                               ⇑
    constructor(first: InfantryUnit,        ⇑ // Delegating
                second: InfantryUnit) : this(first) {
    }
```

But this is clearly not the way to go, since we cannot predict how many more elements Dave may pass us. If you come from Java, you have probably thought about variadic functions already, which can take an arbitrary number of arguments of the same type. In Java, you would declare the parameter as `InfantryUnit... units`.

Kotlin provides us with the `vararg` keyword for the same purposes. Combining those two approaches, we get the following nice piece of code:

```
class Squad(val infantryUnits: MutableList<InfantryUnit> =
mutableListOf()) {

    constructor(vararg units: InfantryUnit) : this(mutableListOf()) {
        for (u in units) {
            this.infantryUnits.add(u)
        }
    }
}
```

Counting bullets

The game designer catches you in the evening, when you are about to go home of course. He wants to add the ammo count for the entire squad so each squad will be able to report how much ammo it has left:

```
fun bulletsLeft(): Long {
    // Do your job
}
```

Where's the catch?

Well, you see, snipers have ammo as separate bullets:

```
class Bullet
```

Riflemen hold their bullets in magazines:

```
class Magazine(capacity: Int) {
    private val bullets = List(capacity) { Bullet() }
}
```

Luckily, you don't have *machine gunners* on your squad yet, because they carry their ammo in belts...

So, you have a complex structure, which may or may not be nested. And you need to perform a certain operation on this structure as a whole. Here's where the Composite design pattern truly comes into play.

You see, the name is a bit confusing. Composite is not so much about composing objects, but more about treating different type objects as nodes of the same tree. For that, they should all implement the same interface.

It may not be that obvious at first. After all, a *rifleman* is clearly not a *squad*. But instead of looking at an interface as an *is-a* relationship, we should look at it as an *ability enabler*. Android, for example, adopts this pattern often.

Our ability is to count bullets:

```
interface CanCountBullets {
    fun bulletsLeft(): Int
}
```

Both Squad and InfantryUnit should implement this interface:

```
interface InfantryUnit : CanCountBullets

class Squad(...) : CanCountBullets {
    ...
}

class Magazine(...): CanCountBullets {
    ...
}
```

And now, since everybody has the same ability, no matter how deep the nesting, we can ask the top-level object to query everything beneath it.

Magazine and Sniper simply count the bullets they contain. The following example shows how we can keep a track of the number of bullets in Magazines:

```
class Magazine(...): CanCountBullets {
    ...
    override fun bulletsLeft() = bullets.size
}
```

The following example shows how we can keep a track of the number of bullets Sniper has:

```
class Sniper(initalBullets: Int = 50) : InfantryUnit {
    private val bullets = List(initalBullets) { Bullet () }
    override fun bulletsLeft() = bullets.size
}
```

For `Rifleman`, we can go over their `Magazines` and check how many bullets they contain:

```
class Rifleman(initialMagazines: Int = 3) : InfantryUnit {
    private val magazines = List<Magazine>(initialMagazines) {
        Magazine(5)
    }

    override fun bulletsLeft(): Int {
        return magazines.sumBy { it.bulletsLeft() }
    }
}
```

Finally, for the squad, we count the sum of counts of all the units squad contains:

```
override fun bulletsLeft(): Int {
    return infantryUnits.sumBy { it.bulletsLeft() }
}
```

Tomorrow, when your product manager discovers suddenly that he needs to implement a platoon (that's a collection of squads), you'll be armed and ready.

Facade

In different implementations and approaches, **Facade** may resemble either an **Adapter** or an **Abstract Factory**.

Its goal seems straightforward—to simplify interacting with another class or a family of classes:

- When we think about *simplifying*, we usually think of the **Adapter** design pattern
- When we think about the *family of classes*, we usually think of an **Abstract Factory**

That's where all the confusion usually comes from. To better understand it, let's go back to the example we used for the Abstract Factory design pattern.

Keep it simple

Let's say that we would like to implement the `loadGame()` method. This method would take a file we already created (we'll discuss how later), or, at the least, the following will be required:

1. At least two HQs will fave to be created (otherwise, the game is already won)
2. Each HQ will have to produce the buildings it had
3. Each building will have to produce the units it had
4. All units will have to magically teleport to the positions they were at when the game was saved
5. If there were any commands given to units (like *obliterating all enemy bases*), they should resume executing them

 We'll discuss how we actually give commands to our units in the next chapter, with the **Command** design pattern. Stay tuned.

Now, usually, it's not just one person working on a game unless it's **Minecraft (TM)**. There's that other guy, Dave, who deals with all the command logic. He's not much into constructing buildings. But in his role, he also needs to load saved games quite often.

As the developer of all those bases that belong to you, you could give him a set of instructions you've written on how the game should be properly loaded. He may or may not follow this set of instructions. Maybe he'll forget to move the units, or build buildings. And the game will crash. You could use the Facade design pattern to simplify the job for him.

What's the main problem Dave has right now?

To load a game, he needs to interact with at least three different interfaces:

- HQ
- Building
- Unit

What he would like is to have only one interface, something like:

```
interface GameWorld
```

That has exactly the methods he needs:

```
fun loadGame(file: File) GameWorld
```

Hey, but that looks like a Static Factory Method there!

Yep, sometimes, design patterns are embedded into one another. We use the Static Factory Method to create our class, but its goal is to be a Facade for other more complex classes. Using a Facade doesn't mean we don't expose interfaces our facade hides behind to the client. Dave can still use every small unit to issue orders after the game is loaded successfully.

Simple, right?

Flyweight

Flyweight is an object without any state. The name comes from *being very light*.

If you've been reading either one of the two previous chapters, you may already think of a type of object that should be very light: a `data` class. But a `data` class is all about state. So, is it related to the Flyweight design pattern at all?

To understand this pattern better, we need to jump back in time some twenty years.

Back in '94, when the original *Design Patterns* book was published, your regular PC had 4 MB of RAM. One of the main goals was to save that precious RAM because you could fit only so much into it.

Nowadays, some cell phones have 4 GB of RAM. Bear that fact in mind when we discuss what the Flyweight design pattern is all about.

Being conservative

Imagine we're building a 2D side-scrolling arcade platformer. That is, you have your character, which you control with arrow keys or a gamepad. Your character can move left, right, and jump.

Since we're a really small indie company consisting of one developer (who is also a graphic designer, product manager, and sales representative), two cats, and a canary named Michael, we use only sixteen colors in our game. And our character is 64 pixels tall and 64 pixels wide. We call him **Maronic**, and that's also the name of our game.

Our character has a lot of enemies, which consist mostly of carnivorous Tanzanian snails:

```
class TansanianSnail
```

Since it's a 2D game, each snail has only two directions of movement—left and right:

```
enum class Direction {
    LEFT,
    RIGHT
}
```

Each snail holds a pair of images and a direction:

```
class TansanianSnail() {
    val directionFacing = Direction.LEFT

    val sprites = listOf(java.io.File("snail-left.jpg"),
                         java.io.File("snail-right.jpg"))
}
```

We can get the current sprite that shows us which direction the snail is facing:

```
fun TansanianSnail.getCurrentSprite() : java.io.File {
    return when (directionFacing) {
        Direction.LEFT -> sprites[0]
        Direction.RIGHT -> sprites[1]
    }
}
```

We can draw it on the screen:

```
      ____
\|_\___  \
/_____/     <-- With a bit of imagination you'll see it's a snail
```

But when it moves, it basically just slides left or right. What we would like is to have three animated sprites to reproduce the snail's movments:

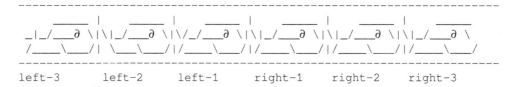

```
left-3     left-2     left-1     right-1     right-2     right-3
```

To have it in our code:

```
val sprites = List(8) { i ->
        java.io.File(when {
                i == 0 -> "snail-left.jpg"
                i == 1 -> "snail-right.jpg"
                i in 2..4 -> "snail-move-left-${i-1}.jpg"
                else -> "snail-move-right${(4-i)}.jpg"
        })
    }
```

We initialize a list of eight elements passing a `block` function as a constructor. For each element, we decide what image to get:

- Positions 0 and 1 are for still images
- Positions 2 through 4 are for moving left
- Positions 5 through 7 are for moving right

Let's do some math now. Each snail is a 64 x 64 image. Assuming each color takes exactly one byte, single images take 4 KB of RAM in the memory. Since we have eight images for a snail, we need 32 KB of RAM for each, which allows us to fit only 32 snails into 1 MB of memory.

Since we want to have thousands of those dangerous and extremely fast creatures on screen, and to be able to run our game on a ten-year-old phone, we clearly need a better solution for that.

Saving memory

What's the problem wehave with our snails? They're actually quite fat, heavyweight snails.

We would like to put them on a diet. Each snail stores eight images within its snaily body. But actually, those images are the same for each snail.

What if we extract those sprites:

```
val sprites = List(8) { i ->
    java.io.File(when {
        i == 0 -> "snail-left.jpg"
        i == 1 -> "snail-right.jpg"
        i in 2..4 -> "snail-move-left-${i-1}.jpg"
        else -> "snail-move-right${(4-i)}.jpg"
    })
}
```

Then we pass this list each time to the `getCurrentSprite()` function:

```
fun TansanianSnail.getCurrentSprite(sprites: List<java.io.File>) :
java.io.File { ... }
```

That way, we'll only consume 256 KB of memory, no matter how many snails we generate. We could generate millions of them without affecting the footprint of our program.

Of course, we should worry about the immutability of the data we pass. That means that at no point in time we should be able to assign `null` to our `sprites` variable as follows:

```
sprites = null
```

That would produce `NullPointerException`. Also, it would be disastrous if someone was to `clear()` this list:

```
sprites.clear()
```

Luckily, Kotlin handles this for us. Since we use `val`, the list is assigned exactly once. Also, since we use List, it produces an immutable list, which cannot be changed or cleared.

All of the preceding lines won't even compile:

```
sprites.clear()
sprites[0] = File("garbage")
sprites[0] = null
```

You still can argue about the usefulness of this pattern nowadays, when memory is plentiful. But, as we already said, the tools in the toolbox don't take much space, and having another design pattern under your belt may still prove useful.

Proxy

This is one misbehaving design pattern. Much like Decorator, it extends object functionality. But, unlike Decorator, which always does at it's told, having a **Proxy** may mean that when asked, the object will do something totally different instead.

A short detour into the RMI world

While discussing Proxy, a lot of sources, mostly related to Java, diverge into discussing another concept, RMI.

RMI in the JVM world stands for Remote Method Invocation, which is a sort of **Remote Procedure Call** (**RPC**). What that means is that you're able to call some code that doesn't exist on your local machine, but sits on some remote machine.

Although a very clever solution, it's very JVM specific, and has become less popular in the era of microservices, where each piece of code may be written in a totally different programming language.

A replacement

When we discussed Creational Patterns, we already discussed the idea of *expensive* objects. For example, an object that accesses network resources, or takes a lot of time to create.

We at **Funny Cat App** (name invented by the canary Michael; remember him from the Flyweight pattern?) provide our users with funny cat images on a daily basis. On our homepage and mobile application, each user sees a lot of thumbnails of funny cats. When he clicks or touches any of those images, it expands to its full-screen glory.

But fetching cat images over the network is very expensive, and it consumes a lot of memory, especially if those are images of cats that tend to indulge themselves in a second dessert after dinner. So, what we would like to do is to have a smart object, something that manages itself.

When the first user access this image, it will be fetched over the network. No way of avoiding that.

But when it's being accessed for the second time, by this or some other user, we would like to avoid going over the network again, and instead return the result that was cached. That's the *misbehaving* part, as we described. Instead of the expected behavior of going over the network each time, we're being a bit lazy, and returning the result that we already prepared. It's a bit like going into a cheap diner, ordering a hamburger, and getting it after only two minutes, but cold. Well, that's because someone else hated onions and returned it to the kitchen a while ago. True story.

That sounds like a lot of logic. But, as you've probably guessed, especially after meeting the Decorator design pattern, Kotlin can perform miracles by reducing the amount of boilerplate code you need to write to achieve your goals:

```
data class CatImage(private val thumbnailUrl: String,
                    private val url: String) {
    val image: java.io.File by lazy {
        // Actual fetch goes here
    }
}
```

As you may notice, we use the `by` keyword to delegate initialization of this field to a standard function called `lazy`.

The first call to `image` will execute a block of our code and save its results into the `image` property.

Sometimes, the Proxy design pattern is divided into three sub-patterns:

- Virtual proxy: Lazily caches the result
- Remote proxy: Issues a call to the remote resource
- Protection or access control proxy: denies access to unauthorized parties

Depending on your views, you can regard our example as either a virtual proxy or a combination of virtual and remote proxies.

Lazy delegation

You may wonder what happens if two threads try to initialize the image at the same time. By default, the `lazy()` function is synchronized. Only one thread will win, and others will wait until the image is ready.

If you don't mind two threads executing the `lazy` block (it's not that expensive, for example), you can use `by lazy(LazyThreadSafetyMode.PUBLICATION)`.

If performance is absolutely critical to you, and you're absolutely sure that two threads won't ever execute the same block simultaneously, you can use `LazyThreadSafetyMode.NONE`.

Summary

In this chapter, we learned how structural design patterns help us to create more flexible code that can adapt to changes with ease, sometimes even at runtime. We've covered **operator overloading** in Kotlin and its limitations. You should know how to create a shortcut to a type name with `typealias` and how to define efficient constants with `const`.

We've covered how delegating to another class works in Kotlin, by implementing the same interface and using the `by` keyword.

In addition, we covered functions that can receive an **arbitrary number of arguments** with `vararg` and **lazy initialization** with `lazy`.

In the next chapter, we'll discuss the third family of classical design patterns: behavioral patterns.

Getting Familiar with Behavioral Patterns 4

This chapter discusses behavioral patterns with Kotlin. Behavioral patterns deal with how objects interact with one another.

We'll see how an object can behave in a totally different manner based on the situation, how objects can communicate without knowledge of one another, and how we can iterate over complex structures easily.

In this chapter, we will cover the following topics:

- Strategy
- Iterator
- State
- Command
- Chain of responsibility
- Interpreter
- Mediator
- Memento
- Visitor
- Template method
- Observer

Strategy

Remember *Maronic,* the platformer we were designing in `Chapter 3`, *Understanding Structural Patterns,* while discussing the **Facade** design pattern?

Well, canary Michael, who acts as a game designer in our small indie game development company, came up with a great idea. What if we were to give our hero an arsenal of weapons to protect us from those horrible carnivorous snails?

Weapons all shoot projectiles (you don't want to get close to those dangerous snails) in the direction our hero is facing:

```
enum class Direction {
    LEFT, RIGHT
}
```

All projectiles should have a pair of coordinates (our game is 2D, remember?) and a direction:

```
abstract class Projectile(private val x: Int,
                          private val y: Int,
                          private val direction: Direction)
```

If we were to shoot only one type of projectile, that would be simple, since we already covered the **Factory** pattern in `Chapter 2`, *Working with Creational Patterns*:

```
class OurHero {
    private var direction = Direction.LEFT
    private var x: Int = 42
    private var y: Int = 173

    fun shoot(): Projectile {
        return object : Projectile(x, y, direction) {
            // Draw and animate projectile here
        }
    }
}
```

But Michael wants our hero to have at least three different weapons:

- **Peashooter**: Shoots small peas that fly straight. Our hero starts with it.
- **Pomegranate**: Explodes when hitting an enemy, much like a grenade.
- **Banana**: Returns like a boomerang when it reaches the end of the screen.

Come on, Michael, give us some slack! Can't you just stick with regular guns that all work the same?!

Fruit arsenal

First, let's discuss how we could solve this in *the Java way*.

In Java, we would have created an interface, that abstracts the changes. In our case, what changes is our hero's weapon:

```
interface Weapon {
    fun shoot(x: Int,
              y: Int,
              direction: Direction): Projectile
}
```

Then all other weapons would implement this interface:

```
class Peashooter : Weapon {
    override fun shoot(x: Int,
                       y: Int,
                       direction: Direction) =
                        object : Projectile(x, y, direction) {
        // Fly straight
    }
}

class Pomegranate : Weapon {
    override fun shoot(x: Int,
                       y: Int,
                       direction: Direction)  =
                        object : Projectile(x, y, direction) {
        // Explode when you hit first enemy
    }
}

class Banana : Weapon {
    override fun shoot(x: Int,
                       y: Int,
                       direction: Direction)  =
                        object : Projectile(x, y, direction) {
        // Return when you hit screen border
    }
}
```

Then our hero would hold a reference to a weapon (`Peashooter` at the beginning):

```
private var currentWeapon : Weapon = Peashooter()
```

It would delegate the actual shooting process to it:

```
fun shoot(): Projectile = currentWeapon.shoot(x, y, direction)
```

What's left is the ability to equip another weapon:

```
fun equip(weapon: Weapon) {
    currentWeapon = weapon
}
```

And that's what the **Strategy** design pattern is all about. Now, our algorithms (Maronic's weapons, in that case) are interchangeable.

Citizen function

With Kotlin, there's a more efficient way to implement the same functionality using fewer classes. That's thanks to the fact that functions in Kotlin are *first-class citizens*.

What does that mean?

For one, we can assign functions to the variables of our class, like any other normal value.

It makes sense that you can assign a primitive value to your variable:

```
val x = 7
```

You could either assign an object to it:

```
var myPet = Canary("Michael")
```

So, why should you be able to assign a function to your variable? As follows:

```
val square = fun (x: Int): Long {
    return (x * x).toLong()
}
```

With Kotlin, this is totally valid.

Switching sides

So, how do higher-order functions help us here?

First, we'll define a namespace for all our weapons. This is not mandatory, but helps to keep everything in check:

```
object Weapons {
    // Functions we'll be there soon
}
```

Then, instead of classes, each of our weapons will become a function:

```
val peashooter = fun(x: Int, y: Int, direction: Direction):
Projectile {
        // Fly straight
}

val banana = fun(x: Int, y: Int, direction: Direction):
    Projectile {
        // Return when you hit screen border
}

val pomegranate = fun(x: Int, y: Int, direction: Direction):
Projectile {
        // Explode when you hit first enemy
}
```

The most interesting part is our hero. It now holds two functions:

```
class OurHero {
    // As before
    var currentWeapon = Weapons.peashooter

    val shoot = fun() {
        currentWeapon(x, y, direction)
    }
}
```

The interchangeable part is `currentWeapon`, while `shoot` is now an anonymous function that wraps it.

To test that our idea works, we can shoot the default weapon once, then switch to `Banana` and shoot it again:

```
val h = OurHero()
h.shoot()
```

```
h.currentWeapon = Weapons.banana
h.shoot()
```

Notice that this dramatically reduces the number of classes we have to write, while keeping the functionality the same.

Iterator

When we were discussing the **Composite** design pattern in the previous chapter, we noted that the design pattern felt a bit incomplete. Now is the time to reunite the twins separated at birth. Much like Arnold Schwarzenegger and Danny DeVito, they're very different, but complement each other well.

One, two... many

We're back to our squads and platoons in our *CatsCraft 2: Revenge of the Dogs* strategy game.

As you may remember from the previous chapter, Squad consists of InfantryUnits:

```
interface InfantryUnit

class Squad(val infantryUnits: MutableList<InfantryUnit> =
mutableListOf()) {
}
```

Each squad should also get a commander now.

The commander of a squad called Sergeant is also an InfantryUnit:

```
class Squad(...) {
    val commander = Sergeant()
}

class Sergeant: InfantryUnit
```

Please disregard the fact that our sergeant doesn't have a name and gets created on the fly. We're two days short of releasing this game and beating the competition. Names are not important now.

The platoon is a collection of squads, and it also has a commander, called `Lieutenant`:

```
class Platoon(val squads: MutableList<Squad> = mutableListOf()) {
    val commander = Lieutenant()
}

class Lieutenant: InfantryUnit
```

What our CEO wants is a platoon, and to be able to know which units it consists of.

So, when we have the following lines in our code:

```
val rangers = Squad("Josh", "Ew    an", "Tom")
val deltaForce = Squad("Sam", "Eric", "William")
val blackHawk = Platoon(rangers, deltaForce)

for (u in blackHawk) {
    println(u)
}
```

We would print by order of seniority:

```
Lieutenant, Sergeant, Josh, Ewan, Tom, ...
```

Nowadays, this task may seem trivial to you, especially if you come from the Java world. But back in '94, data structures were mostly arrays of primitive types. Yes, `Array<Int>`, I'm looking at you.

Iterating over an array wouldn't be that hard, even in Java:

```
int[] array = new int[] {1, 2, 3};
for (int i = 0; i < array.length; i++) {
    System.out.println(i);
}
```

What are we to do with something much more complex?

Running through the values

If you're using an IDE such as IntelliJ, it will give you a hint on what the problem may be:

```
for (u in blackHawk) { <== For-loop range must have an 'iterator()'
method
    // Wanted to do something here
}
```

So, our Platoon needs to have a function called `iterator()`. And since it's a special function, we'll need to use the `operator` keyword.

```
operator fun iterator() = ...
```

What our function returns is an anonymous object that implements the `Iterator<T>` interface:

```
... = object: Iterator<InfantryUnit> {
    override fun hasNext(): Boolean {
        // Are there more objects to iterate over?
    }

    override fun next(): InfantryUnit {
        // Return next InfantryUnit
    }
}
```

The idea behind the iterator design pattern is to separate how the object stores data (in our case, it's something like a tree) and how we can go over this data. As you may know, trees can be iterated in one of two ways:

- depth-first (also known as **depth-first search (DFS)**)
- breadth-first (also known as **breadth-first search (BFS)**)

But do we really care when we need to fetch all the elements?

So, we separate these two concerns: storage aside, repeating aside.

To go over all the elements, we need to implement two methods, one to fetch the next element, and one to let the loop know when to stop.

As an example, we'll implement this object for `Squad`. For Platoon, the logic would be similar, but requires a bit more math.

First, we need a state for our iterator. It will remember that the last element is returned:

```
operator fun iterator() = object: Iterator<InfantryUnit> {
    var i = 0
    // More code here
}
```

Next, we need to tell it when to stop. In our case, the total number of elements is all the units of the squad, plus the sergeant:

```
override fun hasNext(): Boolean {
    return i < infantryUnits.size + 1
}
```

Finally, we need to know which unit to return. If that was the first call, we'll return the sergeant. The next calls will return one of the squad members:

```
override fun next() =
    when (i) {
        0 -> commander
        else -> infantryUnits[i - 1]
    }.also { i++ }
```

 Note that we want to return the next unit, but also to increase our counter. For that, we use the also { } block.

That's only one of the usages of this pattern.

The same object may also have more than one iterator. For example, we could have the second iterator for our squad that would go over elements in reverse order.

To use it, we'll need to call it by name:

```
for (u in deltaForce.reverseIterator()) {
    println(u)
}
```

Since it's just a simple function that returns an iterator now, we don't need the operator keyword:

```
fun reverseIterator() = object: Iterator<InfantryUnit> {
    // hasNext() is same as before
}
```

The only changes are coming in the next() method:

```
override fun next() =
        when (i) {
            infantryUnits.size -> commander
            else -> infantryUnits[infantryUnits.size - i - 1]
        }.also { i++ }
```

Sometimes, it also makes sense to receive an iterator as a parameter for a function:

```
fun <T> printAll(iter: Iterator<T>) {
    while (iter.hasNext()) {
        println(iter.next())
    }
}
```

This function will iterate over anything that supplies an iterator:

```
printAll(deltaForce.iterator())
printAll(deltaForce.reverseIterator())
```

This will print our squad members twice, once in regular and once in reverse order.

As a regular developer who doesn't invent new data structures for his or her living, you may now implement iterators often. But it's important to know how they work behind the scenes nevertheless.

State

You can think of the **State** design pattern as an opinionated Strategy, which we discuss at the beginning of this chapter. But while Strategy is changed from the outside, by the *client*, the State may change internally, based solely on the input it gets.

Look at this dialog a client wrote with Strategy:

> Client: Here's a new thing to do, start doing it from now on.

> Strategy: OK, no problem.

> Client: What I like about you is that you never argue with me.

Compare it with this one:

> Client: Here's some new input I got from you.

> State: Oh, I don't know. Maybe I'll start doing something differently. Maybe not.

The client should also expect that the State may even reject some of its inputs:

> Client: Here's something for you to ponder, State.

> State: I don't know what it is! Don't you see I'm busy? Go bother some Strategy with this!

So, why do clients still tolerate that State of ours? Well, State is really good at keeping everything under control.

Fifty shades of State

Carnivorous snails have had enough of this Maronic hero. He throws peas and bananas at them, only to get to another sorry castle. Now they shall act!

By default, the snail should stand still to conserve snail energy. But when the hero gets close, it dashes towards him aggressively.

If the hero manages to injure it, it should retreat to lick its wounds. Then it will repeat attacking, until one of them is dead.

First, we'll declare what can happen during a snail's life:

```
interface WhatCanHappen {
    fun seeHero()

    fun getHit(pointsOfDamage: Int)

    fun calmAgain()
}
```

Our snail implements this interface, so it can get notified of anything that may happen to it and act accordingly:

```
class Snail : WhatCanHappen {
    private var healthPoints = 10

    override fun seeHero() {
    }

    override fun getHit(pointsOfDamage: Int) {
    }

    override fun timePassed() {
    }
}
```

Now, we declare the Mood class, which we mark with the sealed keyword:

```
sealed class Mood {
    // Some abstract methods here, like draw(), for example
}
```

Sealed classes are abstract and cannot be instantiated. We'll see the benefit of using them in a moment. But before that, let's declare other states:

```
class Still : Mood()

class Aggressive : Mood()

class Retreating : Mood()

class Dead : Mood()
```

Those are all different states, sorry, moods, of our snail.

In State design pattern terms, Snail is the context. It holds the state. So, we declare a member for it:

```
class Snail : WhatCanHappen {
    private var mood: Mood = Still()
    // As before
}
```

Now let's define what Snail should do when it sees our hero:

```
override fun seeHero() {
        mood = when(mood) {
            is Still -> Aggressive()
        }
    }
```

Compilation error! Well, that's where the sealed class comes into play. Much like with an enum, Kotlin knows that there's a finite number of classes that extend from it. So, it requires that our when is exhaustive and specifies all different cases in it.

 If you're using IntelliJ as your IDE, it will even suggest you "add remaining branches" automatically.

Let's describe our state:

```
override fun seeHero() {
    mood = when(mood) {
        is Still -> Aggressive()
        is Aggressive -> mood
        is Retreating -> mood
        is Dead -> mood
    }
}
```

Of course, `else` still works:

```
override fun timePassed() {
    mood = when(mood) {
        is Retreating -> Aggressive()
        else -> mood
    }
}
```

When the snail gets hit, we need to decide if it's dead or not. For that, we can use `when` without an argument:

```
override fun getHit(pointsOfDamage: Int) {
    healthPoints -= pointsOfDamage
    mood = when {
        (healthPoints <= 0) -> Dead()
        mood is Aggressive -> Retreating()
        else -> mood
    }
}
```

Note that we use the `is` keyword, which is the same as `instanceof` in Java, but more concise.

State of the Nation

The previous approach has most of the logic in our *context*. You may sometimes see a different approach, which is valid as your *context* grows bigger.

In this approach, `Snail` would become really thin:

```
class Snail {
    internal var mood: Mood = Still(this)

    private var healthPoints = 10
```

```
    // That's all!
}
```

Note that we marked `mood` as `internal`. That lets other classes in that package alter it.

Instead of `Snail` implementing `WhatCanHappen`, our Mood will:

```
sealed class Mood : WhatCanHappen
```

And now the logic resides within our state objects:

```
class Still(private val snail: Snail) : Mood() {
    override fun seeHero() = snail.mood.run {
            Aggressive(snail)
        }

    override fun getHit(pointsOfDamage: Int) = this
    override fun timePassed() = this
}
```

Note that our state objects now receive a reference to their context in the constructor.

That's the first time we've met the `run` extension function. It's equivalent would be:

```
override fun seeHero(): Mood {
    snail.mood = Aggressive(snail)
    return snail.mood
}
```

By using run, we can preserve the same logic, but omit the function body.

You'll need to decide what approach to use. In our example, this will actually produce much more code, will have to implement all the methods by itself.

Command

This design pattern allows you to encapsulate action inside an object to be executed sometime later.

Furthermore, if we can execute one action later on, why not execute many? Why not schedule exactly when to execute?

That's exactly what we need to do in our *CatsCraft 2: Revenge of the Dogs* game now. Dave, a new developer that we've hired lately, was working hard the whole weekend, while no one was allowed to bother him. He implemented the following abstract methods for our furry soldiers:

```
class Soldier(...)... {
    fun attack(x: Long, y: Long) {
        println("Attacking ($x, $y)")
        // Actual code here
    }

    fun move(x: Long, y: Long) {
        println("Moving to ($x, $y)")
        // Actual code here
    }
}
```

He probably even used the **Bridge** design pattern from the previous chapter to do that.

The problem we need to solve now is that the soldier can remember exactly one *command*. That's it. If he starts at (0, 0), the top of the screen, we first tell him to move(20, 0), that's 20 steps right, and then to move(20, 20), so he'll move straight to (20, 20), and will probably get totally destroyed, because there are dog enemies to avoid at all costs:

```
[cat](0, 0)  ⇒   good direction   ⇒     (20, 0)

      [dog] [dog]                          ⇓
   [dog] [dog] [dog]                        ⇓
      [dog] [dog]
        (5, 20)                         (20, 20)
```

If you've been following this book from the start, or at least joined at Chapter 3, *Understanding Structural Patterns*, you probably have an idea of what we need to do, since we already discussed the concept of *functions as first-class citizens* in the language.

But even if you decided to just figure out how the Command design pattern should work in Kotlin, or opened this book randomly to this section, we'll give you a brief explanation on how that dog obstacle could be solved.

Let's sketch a skeleton for that. We know that we want to hold a list of objects, but we don't know yet what type they should be. So we'll use Any for now:

```
class Soldier {
    private val orders = mutableListOf<Any>()

    fun anotherOrder(action: Any) {
```

```
            this.orders.add(command)
        }
        // More code here
    }
```

Then, we want to iterate over the list and execute the orders we have:

```
class Soldier {
    ...
    // This will be triggered from the outside once in a while
    fun execute() {
        while (!orders.isEmpty()) {
            val action = orders.removeAt(0)
            action.execute() // Compile error for now
        }
    }
    ...
}
```

So, even if you're not familiar with the Command design pattern, you can guess that we can define an interface with a single method, `execute()`:

```
interface Command {
    fun execute()
}
```

And then hold a list of the same time in a member property:

```
private val commands = mutableListOf<Command>()
```

Implement this interface as needed. That's basically what the Java implementation of this pattern would suggest in most cases. But isn't there a better way?

Let's look at the Command again. Its `execute()` method receives nothing, returns nothing, and does something. It's the same as writing the following code then:

```
fun command(): Unit {
    // Some code here
}
```

It's not different at all. We could simplify this further:

```
() -> Unit
```

Instead of having an interface for that called `Command`, we'll have a `typealias`:

```
typealias Command = ()->Unit
```

Now, this line stops compiling again:

```
command.execute() // Unresolved reference: execute
```

Well, that's because `execute()` is just some name we invented. In Kotlin, functions use `invoke()`:

```
command.invoke() // Compiles
```

That's nice, but the functions Dave wrote receive arguments, and our function has no parameters at all.

One option would be to change the signature of our `Command` to receive two parameters:

```
(x: Int, y: Int)->Unit
```

But what if some commands receive no arguments, or only one, or more than two? We also need to remember what to pass to `invoke()` at each step.

A much better way is to have a function generator. That is, a function that returns another function.

If you ever worked with JavaScript language, that's a common practice to use closures to limit the scope and *remember* stuff. We'll do the same:

```
val moveGenerator = fun(s: Soldier,
                        x: Int,
                        y: Int): Command {
    return fun() {
        s.move(x, y)
    }
}
```

When called with proper arguments, `moveGenerator` will return a new function. That function can be invoked whenever we find it suitable, and it will *remember*:

- What method to call
- With which arguments
- On which object

Now, our `Soldier` may have a method like this:

```
fun appendMove(x: Int, y: Int) = apply {
        commands.add(moveGenerator(this, x, y))
}
```

It provides us with a nice fluent syntax:

```
val s = Soldier()
s.appendMove(20, 0)
    .appendMove(20, 20)
    .appendMove(5, 20)
    .execute()
```

This code will print the following:

```
Moving to (20, 0)
Moving to (20, 20)
Moving to (5, 20)
```

Undoing commands

While not directly related, one of the advantages of the Command design pattern is the ability to undo commands. What if we wanted to support such a functionality?

Undoing is usually very tricky, because it involves one of the following:

- Returning to the previous state (impossible if there's more than one client, requires a lot of memory)
- Computing deltas (tricky to implement)
- Defining opposite operations (not always possible)

In our case, the opposite of the command *move from (0,0) to (0, 20)* would be *move from wherever you're now to (0,0)*. This could be achieved by storing a pair of commands:

```
private val commands = mutableListOf<Pair<Command, Command>>()
```

You can also add pairs of commands:

```
fun appendMove(x: Int, y: Int) = apply {
    val oppositeMove = /* If it's the first command, generate move to
current location. Otherwise, get the previous command */
    commands.add(moveGenerator(this, x, y) to oppositeMove)
}
```

Actually, computing the opposite move is quite complex, as we don't save the position of our soldier currently (it was something Dave should have implemented anyway), and we'll also have to deal with some edge cases.

Chain of responsibility

I'm a horrible software architect, and I don't like to speak with people. Hence, while sitting in The Ivory Tower (that's the name of the cafe I often visit), I wrote a small web application. If a developer has a question, he shouldn't approach me directly, oh no. He'll need to send me a proper request through this system, and I shall answer him only if I deem this request worthy.

A filter chain is a very common concept in web servers. Usually, when a request reaches to you, it's expected that:

- Its parameters are already validated
- The user is already authenticated, if possible
- User roles and permissions are known, and the user is authorized to perform an action

So, the code I initially wrote looked something like this:

```
fun handleRequest(r: Request) {
    // Validate
    if (r.email.isEmpty() || r.question.isEmpty()) {
        return
    }
    // Authenticate
    // Make sure that you know whos is this user
    if (r.email.isKnownEmail()) {
        return
    }
    // Authorize
    // Requests from juniors are automatically ignored by architects
    if (r.email.isJuniorDeveloper()) {
        return
    }

    println("I don't know. Did you check StackOverflow?")
}
```

A bit messy, but it works.

Then I noticed that some developers decide they can send me two questions at once. Gotta add some more logic to this function. But wait, I'm an architect, after all. Isn't there a better way to *delegate* this?

This time, we won't learn new Kotlin tricks, but use those that we already learned. We could start with implementing an interface such as this one:

```
interface Handler {
    fun handle(request: Request): Response
}
```

We never discussed what my response to one of the developers looked like. That's because I keep my chain of responsibility so long and complex that usually, they tend to solve problems by themselves. I've never had to answer one of them, quite frankly. But at least we know what their requests look like:

```
data class Request(val email: String, val question: String)

data class Response(val answer: String)
```

Then we could do it the Java way, and start implementing each piece of logic inside its own handler:

```
class BasicValidationHandler(private val next: Handler) : Handler {
    override fun handle(request: Request): Response {
        if (request.email.isEmpty() || request.question.isEmpty()) {
            throw IllegalArgumentException()
        }

        return next.handle(request)
    }
}
```

Other filters would look very similar to this one. We can compose them in any order we want:

```
val req = Request("developer@company.com",
        "Who broke my build?")

val chain = AuthenticationHandler(
            BasicValidationHandler(
                FinalResponseHandler()))

val res = chain.handle(req)

println(res)
```

But I won't even ask you the rhetoric question this time about better ways. Of course there's a better way, we're in the Kotlin world now. And we've seen the usage of functions in the previous section. So, we'll define a function for that task:

```
typealias Handler = (request: Request) -> Response
```

Why have a separate class and interface for something that receives a request and returns a response in a nutshell:

```
val authentication = fun(next: Handler) =
    fun(request: Request): Response {
        if (!request.email.isKnownEmail()) {
            throw IllegalArgumentException()
        }
        return next(request)
    }
```

Here, `authentication` is a function that literally receives a function and returns a function.

Again, we can compose those functions:

```
val req = Request("developer@company.com",
    "Why do we need Software Architects?")

val chain = basicValidation(authentication(finalResponse()))

val res = chain(req)

println(res)
```

It's up to you which method you choose. Using interfaces is more explicit, and would better suit you if you're creating your own library or framework that others may want to extend.

Using functions is more concise, and if you just want to split your code in a more manageable way, it may be the better choice.

Interpreter

This design pattern may seem very simple or very hard, all based on how much background you have in computer science. Some books that discuss classical software design patterns even decide to omit it altogether, or put it somewhere at the end, for curious readers only.

The reason behind this is that the interpreter design pattern deals with translating certain languages. But why would we need that? Don't we have compilers to do that anyway?

We need to go deeper

In this section we discuss that all developers have to speak many languages or sub-languages. Even as regular developers, we use more than one language. Think of tools that build your projects, like Maven or Gradle. You can consider their configuration files, **build scripts**, as languages with specific grammar. If you put elements out of order, your project won't be built correctly. And that's because such projects have interpreters to analyze configuration files and act upon them.

Other examples would be **query languages**, be it one of the SQL variations or one of the languages specific to NoSQL databases.

If you're an Android developer, you may think of XML layouts as such languages too. Even HTML could be considered a language that defines **user interfaces**. And there are others, of course.

Maybe you've worked with one of the **testing frameworks** that define a custom language for testing, such as Cucumber: `github.com/cucumber`.

Each of these examples can be called a **Domain Specific Language** (**DSL**). A language inside a language. We'll discuss how it works in the next section.

A language of your own

In this section, we'll define a simple DSL-for-SQL language. We won't define the format or grammar for it, but only an example of what it should look like:

```
val sql = select("name, age", {
            from("users", {
                where("age > 25")
            }) // Closes from
        }) // Closes select

println(sql) // "SELECT name, age FROM users WHERE age > 25"
```

The goal of our language is to improve readability and prevent some common SQL mistakes, such as typos (like FORM instead of FROM). We'll get compile time validations and autocompletion along the way.

We'll start with the easiest part—`select`:

```
fun select(columns: String, from: SelectClause.()->Unit):
    SelectClause {
    return SelectClause(columns).apply(from)
}
```

 We could write this using single expression notation, but we use the more verbose version for clarity of the example.

This is a function that has two parameters. The first is a `String`, which is simple. The second is another function that receives nothing and returns nothing.

The most interesting part is that we specify the receiver for our lambda:

SelectClause.()->Unit

This is a very smart trick, so be sure to follow along:

SelectClause.()->Unit == (**SelectClause**)->Unit

Although it may seem that this lambda receives nothing, it actually receives one argument, an object of type `SelectClause`.

The second trick lies in the usage of the `apply()` function we've seen before.

Look at this:

```
SelectClause(columns).apply(from)
```

It translates to this:

```
val selectClause = SelectClause(columns)
from(selectClause)
return selectClause
```

Here are the steps the preceding code will perform:

1. Initialize `SelectClause`, which is a simple object that receives one argument in its constructor.
2. Call the `from()` function with an instance of `SelectClause` as its only argument.
3. Return an instance of `SelectClause`.

That code only makes sense if `from()` does something useful with `SelectClause`.

Let's look at our DSL example again:

```
select("name, age", {
    this@select.from("users", {
        where("age > 25")
    })
})
```

We've made the receiver explicit now, meaning that the `from()` function will call the `from()` method on the `SelectClause` object.

You can start guessing what this method looks like. It clearly receives a `String` as its first argument, and another lambda as its second:

```
class SelectClause(private val columns: String) {
    private lateinit var from : FromClause
    fun from(table: String, where: FromClause.()->Unit): FromClause {
        this.from = FromClause(table)
        return this.from.apply(where)
    }
}
```

 This could again be shortened, but then we'd need to use `apply()` within `apply()`, which may seem confusing at this point.

That's the first time we've met the `lateinit` keyword. This keyword is quite dangerous, so use it with some restraint. Remember that the Kotlin compiler is very serious about null safety. If we omit `lateinit`, it will require us to initialize the variable with a default value. But since we'll know it only at a later time, we ask the compiler to relax a bit. Note that if we don't make good on our promises and forget to initialize it, we'll get `UninitializedPropertyAccessException` when first accessing it.

Back to our code; all we do is:

1. Create an instance of `FromClause`
2. Store it as a member of `SelectClause`
3. Pass an instance of `FromClause` to the `where` lambda
4. Return an instance of `FromClause`

Hopefully, you're starting to get the gist of it:

```
select("name, age", {
    this@select.from("users", {
        this@from.where("age > 25")
    })
})
```

What does it mean? After understanding the `from()` method, this should be much simpler. The `FromClause` must have a method called `where()` that receives one argument, of the `String` type:

```
class FromClause(private val table: String) {
    private lateinit var where: WhereClause

    fun where(conditions: String) = this.apply {
        where = WhereClause(conditions)
    }
}
```

Note that we made good on our promise and shortened the method this time.

We initialized an instance of `WhereClause` with the string we received, and returned it. Simple as that:

```
class WhereClause(private val conditions: String) {
    override fun toString(): String {
        return "WHERE $conditions"
    }
}
```

`WhereClause` only prints the word `WHERE` and the conditions it received:

```
class FromClause(private val table: String) {
    // More code here...
    override fun toString(): String {
        return "FROM $table ${this.where}"
    }
}
```

`FromClause` prints the word `FROM` as well as the table name it received, and everything `WhereClause` printed:

```
class SelectClause(private val columns: String) {
    // More code here...
    override fun toString(): String {
        return "SELECT $columns ${this.from}"
```

```
        }
    }
```

`SelectClause` prints the word `SELECT`, the columns it got, and whatever `FromClause` printed.

Taking a break

Kotlin provides beautiful capabilities to create readable and type-safe DSLs. But the interpreter design pattern is one of the hardest in the toolbox. If you didn't get it from the get-go, take some time to debug this code. Understand what `this` means at each step, as well as when we call a function and when we call a method of an object.

Call suffix

In order not to confuse you, we left out one last notion of Kotlin DSL until the end of this section.

Look at this DSL:

```
val sql = select("name, age", {
            from("users", {
                where("age > 25")
            }) // Closes from
        }) // Closes select
```

It could be rewritten as:

```
val sql = select("name, age") {
            from("users") {
                where("age > 25")
            } // Closes from
        } // Closes select
```

This is common practice in Kotlin. If our function receives another function as its last argument, we can pass it out of parentheses.

This results in a much clearer DSL, but may be confusing at first.

Mediator

There's no way around it. The **Mediator** design pattern is simply a control freak. It doesn't like it when one object speaks to the other directly. It gets mad sometimes when that happens. No, everybody should speak only through him. What's his explanation? It reduces coupling between objects. Instead of knowing some other objects, everybody should know only him, the Mediator.

Trouble in the Jungle

Architectural jokes aside, we, the *Maronic* development team, have some real problems. And they're not related to code directly. As you may remember, our little indie company consists of only me, a canary named Michael that acts as a product manager, and two cat designers that sleep most of the day, but do produce some decent mockups from time to time. We have no QA (that's quality assurance guys) whatsoever. Maybe that's one of the reasons our game keeps crashing all the time.

Lately, Michael has introduced me to a parrot named Kenny, who happens to be QA:

```
interface QA {
    fun doesMyCodeWork(): Boolean
}

interface Parrot {
    fun isEating(): Boolean
    fun isSleeping(): Boolean
}

object Kenny : QA, Parrot {
    // Implements interface methods based on parrot schedule
}
```

 This section will use objects for the sake of simplicity.

Parrot QAs are very motivated. They're ready to test the latest version of my game any time. But they really don't like to be bothered when they are either sleeping or eating:

```
class MyMind {
    val qa = Kenny
```

```
        fun taskCompleted() {
            if (!qa.isEating() && !qa.isSleeping()) {
                println(qa.doesMyCodeWork())
            }
        }
    }
```

In case `Kenny` had any questions, I gave him my direct number:

```
    object Kenny : ... {
        val developer = Me
    }
```

`Kenny` was a hard-working parrot. But we had so many bugs that we also had to hire a second parrot QA, Brad. If `Kenny` is free, I give the job to him, as he's more acquainted with our project. But if he's busy, I check if Brad is free, and give this task to him:

```
    class MyMind {
        ...
        val qa2 = Brad

        fun taskCompleted() {
            ...
            else if (!qa2.isEating() && !qa2.isSleeping()) {
                println(qa2.doesMyCodeWork())
            }
        }
    }
```

`Brad`, being more junior, usually checks up with `Kenny` first. And `Kenny` also gave my number to him:

```
    object Brad : QA, Parrot {
        val senior = Kenny
        val developer = Me
        ...
    }
```

Then Brad introduces me to `George`. `George` is an owl, so he sleeps at different times than `Kenny` and Brad. That means that he can check my code at night. The problem is, `George` is an avid football fan. So before calling him, we need to check if he's watching a game now:

```
    class MyMind {
        ...
        val qa3 = George

        fun taskCompleted() {
```

```
    ...
    else if (!qa3.isWatchingFootball()) {
        println(qa3.doesMyCodeWork())
    }
}
}
```

Kenny as a habit checks with George too, because George is a very knowledgeable owl:

```
object Kenny : QA, Parrot {
    val peer = George
    ...
}
```

And George checks with Kenny, because Kenny is also into football, it seems:

```
object George : QA, Owl {
    val mate = Kenny
    ...
}
```

George loves to call me during the night with his questions:

```
object George : QA, Owl {
    val developer = Me
    ...
}
```

Then there's Sandra. She's a different kind of bird, because she's not a QA, but a copywriter:

```
interface Copywriter {
    fun areAllTextsCorrect(): Boolean
}

interface Kiwi

object Sandra : Copywriter, Kiwi {
    override fun areAllTextsCorrect(): Boolean {
        return ...
    }
}
```

I try not to bother her, unless it's a major release:

```
class MyMind {
    ...
    val translator = Sandra
```

```
fun taskCompleted(isMajorRelease: Boolean) {
    ...
    if (isMajorRelease) {
        println(translator.areAllTranslationsCorrect())
    }
}
}
```

OK, now I have a few problems:

- First, my mind almost explodes trying to remember all those names. So might yours.
- Second, I also need to remember how to interact with each one. I'm the one doing all the checks before calling them.
- Third, notice how George tries to confirm everything with Kenny, and Kenny with George? Luckily, up until now, George is always watching a football game when Kenny calls him. And Kenny is asleep when George needs to confirm something with him. Otherwise, they would get stuck on the phone for eternity...
- Fourth, and what bothers me the most, is that Kenny plans to leave soon to open his own startup, ParrotPi. Imagine all the code we'll have to change now!

All I want to do is to check if everything is alright with my code. Someone else should do all this talking!

The middleman

So, I decided that Michael should manage all those processes:

```
interface Manager {
    fun isAllGood(majorRelease: Boolean): Boolean
}
```

Only he will know all the other *birds*:

```
object Michael: Canary, Manager {
    private val kenny = Kenny(this)
    // And all the others
    ...

    override fun isAllGood(majorRelease: Boolean): Boolean {
        if (!kenny.isEating() && !kenny.isSleeping()) {
            println(kenny.doesMyCodeWork())
        }
        // And all the other logic I had in MyMind
```

```
        ...
    }
}
```

I'll remember only him, and he'll do the rest:

```
class MyPeacefulMind(private val manager: Manager) {
    fun taskCompleted(isMajorRelease: Boolean) {
        println(manager.isAllGood(isMajorRelease))
    }
}
```

I'll also change my phone number, and make sure that everybody gets only Michael's:

```
class Brad(private val manager: Manager) : ... {
    // No reference to Me here
    ...
}
```

Now, if somebody needs somebody else's opinion, they need to go through Michael first.

```
class Kenny(private val manager: Manager) : ... {
    // No reference to George, or anyone else
    ...
}
```

Flavors

There are two *flavors* to Mediator. We'll call them *strict* and *loose*. The strict version we've seen previously. We tell Mediator exactly what to do, and expect an answer from it.

The *loose* version will expect us to notify Mediator of what happened, but not to expect an immediate answer. Instead, if he needs to notify us in return, he should call us instead.

Caveats

Michael suddenly becomes ever so important. Everybody knows only him, and only he can manage their interactions. He may even become a *God Object*, all-knowing and almighty, which is an antipattern from Chapter 9, *Designed for Concurrency*. Even if he's so important, be sure to define what this Mediator should, and, even more importantly, what it shouldn't, do.

Memento

Since Michael became a manager, it's been very hard to catch him if I have a question. And when I do ask him something, he just throws something and runs to the next meeting.

Yesterday, I asked him what the next weapon we would introduce in our *Maronic* game should be. He told me it should be a Coconut Cannon, clear as day. But today, when I presented him with this feature, he chirped at me angrily! He said he told me to implement a Pineapple Launcher instead. I'm lucky he's just a canary still...

But it would be great if I could just record him, and when we have another meeting that goes awry because he's not paying full attention, I would just replay everything he said.

Remembrance

Summing up my problems first—Michael's thoughts are his and his only:

```
class Manager {
    private var lastThought = "Should get some coffee"
    private var repeatThat = 3
    private var thenHesitate = "Or maybe tea?"
    private var secretThought = "No, coffee it is"
    ...
}
```

Moreover, they're quite complex and scattered. I have no access to them, but only to their byproduct:

```
class Manager {
    ...
    fun whatAreYouThinking() {
        for (i in 1..repeatThat) {
            println(lastThought)
        }
        println(thenHesitate)
    }
    ...
}
```

Even recording what he says is quite hard (because he doesn't return anything).

And even if I did record him, Michael can claim it's what he said, not what he meant:

Why did you bring me tea? I wanted coffee!

The solution may seem quite obvious. Let's use an inner class, thought, that will capture this last thought:

```
class Manager {
    . . .
    class Thought {
        fun captureThought(): CapturedThought {
            return CapturedThought(lastThought,
                                   repeatThat,
                                   thenHesitate,
                                   secretThought)
        }
    }

    data class CapturedThought(val thought: String,
                               val repeat: Int,
                               val hesitate: String,
                               val secret: String)
}
```

The only problem is that this code doesn't compile. It's because we're missing a new keyword, inner, to mark our class. If we omit this keyword, the class is called Nested, and is similar to the static nested class from Java.

Now we can *record* what Michael says at this moment:

```
val michael = Manager()

val captured = michael.Thought().captureThought()
```

Let's assume that Michael changes his mind at some point. We'll add another function for that:

```
class Manager {
    . . .
    fun anotherThought() {
        lastThought = "Tea would be better"
        repeatThat = 2
        thenHesitate = "But coffee is also nice"
        secretThought = "Big latte would be great"
    }
}
michael.anotherThought()
```

We can always repeat the thought that we captured:

```
michael.whatAreYouThinking()
```

This will print:

Tea would be better
Tea would be better
But coffee is also nice

Let's check what we've captured:

```
println(captured)
```

This will print:

```
CapturedThought(thought=Should get some coffee, repeat=3, hesitate=Or maybe
tea?, secret=No, coffee it is)
```

We can even rewind Michael's thoughts if he would allow it:

```
class Manager {
    ...
    inner class Thought {
        ...
        fun rewindThought(val previousThought: CapturedThought) {
            with(previousThought) {
                lastThought = thought
                repeatThat = repeat
                thenHesitate = hesitate
                secretThought = secret
            }
        }
    }
    ...
}
```

Note how here we use the `with` standard function to avoid repeating `previousThought` on each line.

Visitor

This design pattern is usually a close friend of the **Composite** design pattern that we discussed in Chapter 3, *Understanding Structural Patterns*. It can either extract data from a complex tree-like structure or add behavior to each node of the tree, much like the **Decorator** design pattern.

So, my plan, being a lazy software architect, worked out quite well. Both my mail-sending system from **Builder** and my request-answering system from **Chain of Responsibility** worked quite well. But some developers still begin to suspect that I'm a bit of a fraud.

To confuse them, I plan to produce weekly emails with links to all the latest buzzword articles. Of course, I don't plan to read them myself, just collect them from some popular technology sites.

Writing a crawler

Let's look at the following structure, which is very similar to what we had when discussing the **Iterator** design pattern:

```
Page(Container(Image(),
                Link(),
                Image())),
     Table(),
     Link(),
     Container(Table(),
               Link()),
     Container(Image(),
               Container(Image(),
                         Link()))))
```

The Page is a container for other HtmlElements, but not HtmlElement by itself. Container holds other containers, tables, links, and images. Image holds its link in the src attribute. Link has the href attribute instead.

We start by creating a function that will receive the root of our object tree, a Page in this case, and return a list of all available links:

```
fun collectLinks(page: Page): List<String> {
    // No need for intermediate variable there
    return LinksCrawler().run {
        page.accept(this)
```

```
            this.links
    }
}
```

Using `run` allows us to control what we return from the block body. In this case, we would return the `links` we've gathered.

In Java, the suggested way to implement the **Visitor** design pattern is to add a method for each class that would accept our new functionality. We'll do the same, but not for all classes. Instead, we'll define this method only for container elements:

```
private fun Container.accept(feature: LinksCrawler) {
    feature.visit(this)
}

// Same as above but shorter
private fun Page.accept(feature: LinksCrawler) = feature.visit(this)
```

Our feature will need to hold a collection internally, and expose it only for read purposes. In Java, we would specify only the getter and no setter for that member. In Kotlin, we can specify the value without a backing field:

```
class LinksCrawler {
    private var _links = mutableListOf<String>()

    val links
        get()= _links.toList()
    ...
}
```

We wish for our data structure to be immutable. That's the reason we're calling `toList()` on it.

 The functions that iterate over branches could be further simplified if we use the **Iterator** design pattern.

For containers, we simply pass their elements further:

```
class LinksCrawler {
    ...
    fun visit(page: Page) {
        visit(page.elements)
    }
```

```
    fun visit(container: Container) = visit(container.elements)
    ...
}
```

Specifying the parent class as `sealed` helps the compiler further:

```
sealed class HtmlElement

class Container(...) : HtmlElement(){
    ...
}

class Image(...) : HtmlElement() {
    ...
}

class Link(...) : HtmlElement() {
    ...
}

class Table : HtmlElement()
```

The most interesting logic is in the leaves:

```
class LinksCrawler {
    ...
    private fun visit(elements: List<HtmlElement>) {
        for (e in elements) {
            when (e) {
                is Container -> e.accept(this)
                is Link -> _links.add(e.href)
                is Image -> _links.add(e.src)
                else -> {}
            }
        }
    }
}
```

Note that in some cases, we don't want to do anything. That's specified by an empty block in our else: `else -> {}`.

That's the first time we've seen **smart casts** in Kotlin.

Notice that after we checked that the element is a `Link`, we gained type-safe access to its `href` attribute. That's because the compiler is doing the casts for us. The same holds true for the `Image` element as well.

Although we achieved our goals, the usability of this pattern can be argued. As you can see, it's one of the more verbose elements, and introduces tight coupling between classes receiving additional behavior and Visitor itself.

Template method

Some lazy people make art out of their laziness. Take me for example. Here's my daily schedule:

1. 8:00–9:00: Arrive at the office
2. 9:00–10:00: Drink coffee
3. 10:00–12:00: Attend some meetings or review code
4. 12:00–13:00: Go out for lunch
5. 13:00–16:00: Attend some meetings or review code
6. 16:00: Sneak out home

As you can see, some of the parts of the schedule never change, and some do. At first, I thought I could *decorate* my changing schedule with that `setup` and `teardown` logic, which happens *before* and *after*. But then there's lunch, which is holy for architects and happens *in between*.

Java is pretty clear on what you should do. First, you create an abstract class. All methods that you want to implement by yourself you mark as private:

```
abstract class DayRoutine {
    private fun arriveToWork() {
        println("Hi boss! I appear in the office sometimes!")
    }

    private fun drinkCoffee() {
        println("Coffee is delicious today")
    }

    ...

    private fun goToLunch() {
        println("Hamburger and chips, please!")
    }

    ...

    private fun goHome() {
```

```
        // Very important no one notices me
        println()
    }


    ...

}
```

For all methods that are changing from day to day, you define an abstract:

```
abstract class DayRoutine {
    ...
    abstract fun doBeforeLunch()
    ...
    abstract fun doAfterLunch()
    ...
}
```

If you allow the changing of a method, but want to provide a default implementation, you leave it public:

```
abstract class DayRoutine {
    ...
    open fun bossHook() {
        // Hope he doesn't hook me there
    }
    ...
}
```

And finally, you have a method that executes your algorithm. It's final by default:

```
abstract class DayRoutine {
    ...
    fun runSchedule() {
        arriveToWork()
        drinkCoffee()
        doAfterLunch()
        goToLunch()
        doAfterLunch()
        goHome()
    }
}
```

If we now want to have a schedule for Monday, we simply implement the missing parts:

```
class MondaySchedule : DayRoutine() {
    override fun doBeforeLunch() {
        println("Some pointless meeting")
        println("Code review. What this does?")
```

```
    }

    override fun doAfterLunch() {
        println("Meeting with Ralf")
        println("Telling jokes to other architects")
    }

    override fun bossHook() {
        println("Hey, can I have you for a sec in my office?")
    }
}
```

What does Kotlin add on top of that? What it usually does—conciseness. As we've seen previously, this can be achieved through functions.

We have three *moving parts*—two mandatory activities (the software architect must do something before and after lunch) and one optional (the boss may stop him before he sneaks off home or not):

```
fun runSchedule(beforeLunch: ()->Unit,
                afterLunch: ()->Unit,
                bossHook: (()->Unit)? = fun() { println() }) {
    ...
}
```

We'll have a function that accepts up to three other functions as its arguments. The first two are mandatory, and the third may not be supplied at all, or assigned with `null` to explicitly state that we don't want that function to happen:

```
fun runSchedule(...) {
    ...
    arriveToWork()
    drinkCoffee()
    beforeLunch()
    goToLunch()
    afterLunch()
    bossHook?.let { it() }
    goHome()
}
```

Inside this function, we'll have our algorithm. Invocations of `beforeLunch()` and `afterLunch()` should be clear; after all, those are the functions that are passed to us as arguments. The third one, bossHook, may be null, so we execute it only if it's not: `?.let { it() }`.

But what about the other functions, those we want to always implement by ourselves? Kotlin has a notion of local functions. Those are functions that reside in other functions:

```
fun runSchedule(...) {
    fun arriveToWork(){
        println("How are you all?")
    }

    val drinkCoffee = { println("Did someone left the milk out?") }

    fun goToLunch() = println("I would like something italian")

    val goHome = fun () {
        println("Finally some rest")
    }

    arriveToWork()
    drinkCoffee()
    ...
    goToLunch()
    ...
    goHome()
}
```

Those are all valid ways to declare a local function. No matter how you define them, they're invoked in the same way.

We're left with the same result, as you can see. Define the algorithm structure, but let others decide what to do at some points: that's what the Template Method is all about.

Observer

Probably one of the highlights of this chapter, this design pattern will provide us with a bridge to the following chapters, dedicated to functional programming.

So, what is Observer pattern about? You have one *publisher*, which may also be called a *subject*, that may have many *subscribers*, which may also be called *observers*. Each time something interesting happens with the publisher, it should update all of its subscribers.

This may look a lot like the Mediator design pattern, but there's a twist. Subscribers should be able to register or unregister themselves at runtime.

In the classical implementation, all subscribers/observers need to implement a certain interface in order for the publisher to be able to update them. But since Kotlin has higher-order functions, we can omit this part. The publisher will still have to provide means for observers to be able to subscribe and unsubscribe.

Animal Choir

So, animals have decided to have a choir of their own. The cat was elected as the conductor of the choir (it didn't like to sing anyway).

The problem is that animals escaped from the Java world, and don't have a common interface. Instead, each has a different method to make a sound:

```kotlin
class Bat {
    fun screech() {
        println("Eeeeeee")
    }
}

class Turkey {
    fun gobble() {
        println("Gob-gob")
    }
}

class Dog {
    fun bark() {
        println("Woof")
    }

    fun howl() {
        println("Auuuu")
    }
}
```

Luckily, the cat was elected not only because it was vocally challenged, but also because it was smart enough to follow this chapter until now. So it knows that in the Kotlin world, it can accept functions:

```kotlin
class Cat {
    ...
    fun joinChoir(whatToCall: ()->Unit) {
        ...
    }
}
```

```
fun leaveChoir(whatNotToCall: ()->Unit) {
    ...
}
...
}
```

Previously, we've seen how to pass a new function as an argument, as well as passing a literal function. But how do we pass a reference to a member function?

That's what member reference operator is for—: : :

```
val catTheConductor = Cat()

val bat = Bat()
val dog = Dog()
val turkey = Turkey()

catTheConductor.joinChoir(bat::screech)
catTheConductor.joinChoir(dog::howl)
catTheConductor.joinChoir(dog::bark)
catTheConductor.joinChoir(turkey::gobble)
```

Now the cat needs to save all those subscribers somehow. Luckily, we can put them on a map. What would be the key? It could be the function itself:

```
class Cat {
    private val participants = mutableMapOf<()->Unit, ()->Unit>()

    fun joinChoir(whatToCall: ()->Unit) {
        participants.put(whatToCall, whatToCall)
    }
    ...
}
```

 If all those ()->Unit instances are making you dizzy, be sure to use typealias to give them more semantic meaning, such as subscriber.

The bat decides to leave the choir. After all, no one is able to hear its beautiful singing anyway:

```
class Cat {
    ...
    fun leaveChoir(whatNotToCall: ()->Unit) {
        participants.remove(whatNotToCall)
    }
}
```

```
    ...
}
```

All `Bat` needs to do is to pass its subscriber function again:

```
catTheConductor.leaveChoir(bat::screech)
```

That's the reason we used the map in the first place. Now `Cat` can call all its choir members and tell them to sing. Well, produce sounds:

```
typealias Times = Int

class Cat {
    ...
    fun conduct(n: Times) {
        for (p in participants.values) {
            for (i in 1..n) {
                p()
            }
        }
    }
}
```

The rehearsal went well. But `Cat` feels very tired after doing all those loops. It would rather delegate the job to choir members. That's not a problem at all:

```
class Cat {
    private val participants = mutableMapOf<(Int)->Unit, (Int)->Unit>()

    fun joinChoir(whatToCall: (Int)->Unit) {
        ...
    }

    fun leaveChoir(whatNotToCall: (Int)->Unit) {
        ...
    }

    fun conduct(n: Times) {
        for (p in participants.values) {
            p(n)
        }
    }
}
```

Our subscribers all look like turkeys here:

```
class Turkey {
    fun gobble(repeat: Times) {
        for (i in 1..repeat) {
            println("Gob-gob")
        }
    }
}
```

Actually, it is a bit of a problem. What if the Cat was to tell each animal what sound to make: high or low? We'll have to change all subscribers again, and the Cat too.

While designing your publisher, pass single data classes with many properties, instead of sets of data classes or other types. That way, you'll have to refactor your subscribers less, in case new properties are added:

```
enum class SoundPitch {HIGH, LOW}
data class Message(val repeat: Times, val pitch: SoundPitch)

class Bat {
    fun screech(message: Message) {
        for (i in 1..message.repeat) {
            println("${message.pitch} Eeeeeee")
        }
    }
}
```

 Make sure that your messages are immutable. Otherwise, you may experience strange behavior!

What if you have sets of different messages you're sending from the same publisher?

Use smart casts:

```
interface Message {
    val repeat: Times
    val pitch: SoundPitch
}

data class LowMessage(override val repeat: Times) : Message {
    override val pitch = SoundPitch.LOW
}

data class HighMessage(override val repeat: Times) : Message {
```

```
            override val pitch = SoundPitch.HIGH
    }

    class Bat {
        fun screech(message: Message) {
            when (message) {
                is HighMessage -> {
                    for (i in 1..message.repeat) {
                        println("${message.pitch} Eeeeeee")
                    }
                }
                else -> println("Can't :(")
            }
        }
    }
}
```

Summary

That was a long chapter. But we've also learned a lot. We finished covering all classical design patterns, including eleven behavioral ones. In Kotlin, functions can be passed to other functions, returned from functions, and assigned to variables. That's what the "functions as first-class citizens" concept is all about. If your class is all about behavior, it often makes sense to replace it with a function. Iterator is yet another `operator` in the language. Sealed classes help in making `when` statements exhaustive. The `run` extension function allows for controlling what will be returned from it. A lambda with a receiver allows more clear syntax in your DSLs. Another keyword, `lateinit`, tells the compiler to relax a bit in its null safety checks. Use with care! And finally, we covered how to reference an existing method with `::`.

In the next chapter, we'll move on from an object-oriented programming paradigm with its well-known design patterns to another paradigm—functional programming.

5
Functional Programming

In this chapter, we're going to discuss basic principles of functional programming, and how they fit into the Kotlin programming language. We won't introduce much new syntax, as you'll soon see. It would have been hard to discuss benefits of the language in the previous chapters without touching on concepts such as *data immutability* and *functions as first-class values*. But, as we did before, we'll look at those features from a different angle: not how to use them to implement well-known design patterns in a better way, but their purpose.

In this chapter, we will cover the following topics:

- Why functional programming?
- Immutability
- Functions as values
- Expressions, not statements
- Recursion

Why functional programming?

Functional programming has been around for almost as long as other programming paradigms, such as procedural and object-oriented programming, if not longer. But in the past 10 years, it has gained major momentum. The reason for that is because something else stalled: CPU speeds. We cannot speed up our CPUs as much as we did in the past, so we must parallelize our programs. And it turns out that the functional programming paradigm is exceptional at running parallel tasks.

The evolution of multicore processors is a very interesting topic by itself, but we'll be able to cover it only briefly. Workstations had multiple processors since the 1980s at least, to support running tasks from different users in parallel. Since workstations were huge anyway, they didn't need to worry about cramming everything into one chip. But with multiprocessors coming to the consumer market around 2005, it was necessary to have one physical unit that could do work in parallel. That's the reason we have multiple cores on one chip in our PC or laptop.

But that's not the only reason some swear by functional programming. Here are a few more:

- Functional programming favors pure functions, and pure functions are usually easier to reason about and to test
- Code written in a functional way is often more declarative than imperative, dealing with the *what* and not the *how*

Immutability

One of the key concepts of functional programming is immutability. It means that from the moment the function receives input to the moment the function returns output, the object doesn't change. How could it change, you wonder? Let's see a simple example:

```
fun <T> printAndClear(list: MutableList<T>) {
    for (e in list) {
        println(e)
        list.remove(e)
    }
}
printAndClear(mutableListOf("a", "b", "c"))
```

The output would be first `"a"`, then we'll receive `ConcurrentModificationException`.

Wouldn't it be great if we could protect ourselves from such runtime exceptions in the first place?

Tuples

In functional programming, a tuple is a piece of data that cannot be changed after it is created. One of the most basic tuples in Kotlin is Pair:

```
val pair = "a" to 1
```

Pair contains two properties, first and second, and is immutable:

```
pair.first = "b" // Doesn't work
pair.second = 2  // Still doesn't
```

We can destructure a Pair into two separate values:

```
val (key, value) = pair
println("$key => $value")
```

When iterating over a map, we receive another tuple, `Map.Entry`:

```
for (p in mapOf(1 to "Sunday", 2 to "Monday")) {
    println("${p.key} ${p.value}")
}
```

In general, *data classes* are usually a good implementation for tuples. But, as we'll see in the *Value Mutation* section, not every data class is a proper tuple.

Value mutation

In Maronic, we would like to count the average score over one thousand games. For that, we have the following data class:

```
data class AverageScore(var totalScore: Int = 0,
                        var gamesPlayed: Int = 0) {
    val average: Int
        get() = if (gamesPlayed <= 0)
                    0
                else
                    totalScore / gamesPlayed
}
```

We were smart: we protected ourselves from any invalid output by checking for divisions by zero.

But what will happen when we write the following code?

```
val counter = AverageScore()

thread(isDaemon = true) {
    while(true) counter.gamesPlayed = 0
}

for (i in 1..1_000) {
    counter.totalScore += Random().nextInt(100)
```

```
    counter.gamesPlayed++

    println(counter.average)
}
```

Soon enough, you'll receive `ArithmeticException` anyway. Our counter somehow becomes zero.

If you want your data classes to be immutable, be sure to specify all their properties as `val` (values), and not `var` (variables).

Immutable collections

I think that our junior developer learned their lesson. Instead, they produced this code, which is not very efficient, but which gets rid of those variables:

```
data class ScoreCollector(val scores: MutableList<Int> = mutableListOf())

val counter = ScoreCollector()

for (i in 1..1_000) {
    counter.scores += Random().nextInt(100)

    println(counter.scores.sumBy { it } / counter.scores.size)
}
```

But the maleficent thread strikes again:

```
thread(isDaemon= true, name="Maleficent") {
    while(true) counter.scores.clear()
}
```

We again receive `ArithmeticException`.

It's not enough that your data class contains only values. If its value is a collection, it must be immutable in order for the data class to be considered immutable. The same rule is applied to classes contained within other data classes:

```
data class ImmutableScoreCollector(val scores: List<Int>)
```

Now the maleficent thread cannot even call `clear()` on this collection. But how should we add scores to it?

One option is to pass the entire list in the constructor:

```
val counter = ImmutableScoreCollector(List(1_000) {
    Random().nextInt(100)
})
```

Functions as values

We already covered some of the functional capabilities of Kotlin in the chapters dedicated to Design Patterns. The **Strategy** and **Command** design patterns are but a few that heavily rely on the ability to accept functions as arguments, return functions, store them as values, or put them inside collections. In this section, we'll cover some other aspects of functional programming in Kotlin, such as function purity and currying.

Higher-order functions

As we discussed previously, in Kotlin, it's possible for a function to return another function:

```
fun generateMultiply(): (Int, Int) -> Int {
    return { x: Int, y: Int -> x * y}
}
```

Functions can also be assigned to a variable or value to be invoked later on:

```
val multiplyFunction = generateMultiply()
...
println(multiplyFunction(3, 4))
```

The function assigned to a variable is usually called a *literal function*. It's also possible to specify a function as a parameter:

```
fun mathInvoker(x: Int, y: Int, mathFunction: (Int, Int) -> Int) {
    println(mathFunction(x, y))
}

mathInvoker(5, 6, multiplyFunction)
```

If a function is the last parameter, it can also be supplied ad hoc, outside of the brackets:

```
mathInvoker(7, 8) { x, y ->
  x * y
}
```

In general, a function without a name is called an *anonymous* function. If a function without a name uses short syntax, it's called a lambda:

```
val squareAnonymous = fun(x: Int) = x * x
val squareLambda = {x: Int -> x * x}
```

Pure functions

A pure function is a function without any side effects. Take the following function, for example:

```
fun sayHello() {
    println("Hello")
}
```

How do you test to see whether "Hello" is indeed printed? The task is not as simple as it seems, as we'll need some means to capture the standard output, the same console where we usually see stuff printed.

Compare it to the following function:

```
fun hello() = "Hello"
```

The following function doesn't have any side effects. That makes it a lot easier to test:

```
fun testHello(): Boolean {
    return "Hello" == hello()
}
```

Does the `hello()` function look a bit meaningless to your eyes? That's actually one of the properties of pure functions. Their invocation could be replaced by their result (if we knew all their results, that is). This is often called *referential transparency*.

Not every function written in Kotlin is pure:

```
fun <T> removeFirst(list: MutableList<T>): T {
    return list.removeAt(0)
}
```

If we call the function twice on the same list, it will return different results:

```
val list = mutableListOf(1, 2, 3)

println(removeFirst(list)) // Prints 1
println(removeFirst(list)) // Prints 2
```

Try this one:

```
fun <T> withoutFirst(list: List<T>): T {
    return ArrayList(list).removeAt(0)
}
```

Now our function is totally predictable, no matter how many times we invoke it:

```
val list = mutableListOf(1, 2, 3)

println(withoutFirst(list)) // It's 1
println(withoutFirst(list)) // Still 1
```

As you can see, we used an immutable interface this time, List<T>, which helps us by preventing even the possibility of mutating our input. Together with immutable values from the previous section, pure functions provide a very strong tool that allows easier testing by providing predictable results and parallelization of our algorithms.

Currying

Currying is a way to translate a function that takes a number of arguments into a chain of functions that each take a single argument. This may sound confusing, so let's look at a simple example:

```
fun subtract(x: Int, y: Int): Int {
    return x - y
}
println(subtract(50, 8))
```

This is a function that returns two arguments. The result is quite obvious. But maybe we would like to invoke this function with the following syntax instead:

```
subtract(50)(8)
```

We've already seen how we can return a function from another function:

```
fun subtract(x: Int): (Int) -> Int {
    return fun(y: Int): Int {
        return x - y
    }
}
```

Here it is in the shorter form:

```
fun subtract(x: Int) = fun(y: Int): Int {
    return x + y
}
```

And here it is in an even shorter form:

```
fun subtract(x: Int) = {y: Int -> x - y}
```

Although not very useful by itself, it's still an interesting concept to grasp. And if you're a JavaScript developer looking for a new job, make sure you understand it really well, since it's being asked about in nearly every interview.

Memoization

If our function always returns the same output for the same input, we could easily map between previous input and output, and use it as a cache. That technique is called *memoization*:

```
class Summarizer {
    private val resultsCache = mutableMapOf<List<Int>, Double>()

    fun summarize(numbers: List<Int>): Double {
        return resultsCache.computeIfAbsent(numbers, ::sum)
    }

    private fun sum(numbers: List<Int>): Double {
        return numbers.sumByDouble { it.toDouble() }
    }
}
```

We use a method reference operator, `::`, to tell `computeIfAbsent` to use the `sum()` method in the event that input wasn't cached yet.

Note that `sum()` is a pure function, while `summarize()` is not. The latter will behave differently for the same input. But that's exactly what we want in this case:

```
val l1 = listOf(1, 2, 3)
val l2 = listOf(1, 2, 3)
val l3 = listOf(1, 2, 3, 4)

val summarizer = Summarizer()

println(summarizer.summarize(l1)) // Computes, new input
```

```
println(summarizer.summarize(l1)) // Object is the same, no compute
println(summarizer.summarize(l2)) // Value is the same, no compute
println(summarizer.summarize(l3)) // Computes
```

The combination of immutable objects, pure functions, and plain old classes provides us with a powerful tool for performance optimizations. Just remember, nothing is free. We only trade one resource, CPU time, for another resource, memory. And it's up to you to decide which resource is more expensive for you in each case.

Expressions, not statements

A statement is a block of code that doesn't return anything. An expression, on the other hand, returns a new value. Since statements produce no results, the only way for them to be useful is to mutate state. And functional programming tries to avoid mutating the state as much as possible. Theoretically, the more we rely on expressions, the more our functions will be pure, with all the benefits of functional purity.

We've used the `if` expression many times already, so one of its benefits should be clear: it's less verbose and, for that reason, less error-prone than the `if` statement.

Pattern matching

The concept of pattern matching is like `switch/case` on steroids for someone who comes from Java. We've already seen how `when` expression can be used, in `Chapter 1`, *Getting Started with Kotlin*, so let's briefly discuss why this concept is important for the functional paradigm.

As you may know, `switch` in Java accepts only some primitive types, strings, or enums.

Consider the following code in Java:

```
class Cat implements Animal {
    public String purr() {
        return "Purr-purr";
    }
}

class Dog implements Animal {
    public String bark() {
        return "Bark-bark";
    }
```

```
    }

    interface Animal {}
```

If we were to decide which of the functions to call, we would need something like this:

```java
public String getSound(Animal animal) {
    String sound = null;
    if (animal instanceof Cat) {
        sound = ((Cat)animal).purr();
    }
    else if (animal instanceof Dog) {
        sound = ((Dog)animal).bark();
    }

    if (sound == null) {
        throw new RuntimeException();
    }
    return sound;
}
```

This method could be shortened by introducing multiple returns, but in real projects, multiple returns are usually bad practice.

Since we don't have a `switch` statement for classes, we need to use an `if` statement instead.

Compare that with the following Kotlin code:

```kotlin
fun getSound(animal: Animal) = when(animal) {
    is Cat -> animal.purr()
    is Dog -> animal.bark()
    else -> throw RuntimeException()
}
```

Since `when` is an expression, we avoided the intermediate variable altogether. But what's more, using pattern matching, we can also avoid most of the code that concerns type checks and casts.

Recursion

Recursion is a function invoking itself with new arguments:

```kotlin
fun sumRec(i: Int, numbers: List<Int>): Long {
    return if (i == numbers.size) {
```

```
        0
    } else {
        numbers[i] + sumRec(i + 1, numbers)
    }
}
```

We usually avoid recursion, due to **Stack Overflow** error that we may receive if our call stack is too deep. You can call this function with a list that contains a million numbers to experience it:

```
val numbers = List(1_000_000) {it}
println(sumRec(0,  numbers)) // Crashed pretty soon, around 7K
```

One of the great benefits of tail recursion is that it avoids the dreaded stack overflow exception.

Let's rewrite our recursive function using a new keyword, `tailrec`, to avoid that problem:

```
tailrec_fun sumRec(i: Int, sum: Long, numbers: List<Int>): Long {
    return if (i == numbers.size) {
        return sum
    } else {
        sumRec(i+1, numbers[i] + sum, numbers)
    }
}
```

Now the compiler will optimize our call and avoid exception completely.

Summary

You should now have a better understanding of functional programming and its benefits. We've discussed the concepts of immutability and pure functions. A combination of the two often results in more testable code, which is easier to maintain.

Currying and memoization are two useful patterns that originate from functional programming.

Kotlin has a `tailrec` keyword that allows the compiler to optimize *tail recursion*. We also looked at higher-order functions, expressions versus statements, and pattern matching.

In the next chapter, we'll put this knowledge to practical use, and discover how reactive programming builds upon functional programming in order to create scalable and resilient systems.

6
Streaming Your Data

In this chapter, we'll discuss higher-order functions for collections. For Java developers, they first appeared in Java 8 with the introduction of Stream API. But they were around for much longer in functional languages.

First, since we expect that many of our readers are familiar with Java 8, let's cover what Stream API is in Java briefly.

Streams from Java8 are not to be confused with some of the I/O classes with similar names, such as `InputStream` or `OutputStream`. While the latter represent data, the former are sequences of elements of the same type.

If those are sequences, and they all have the same type, how are they different from `Lists`? Well, streams can be infinite, unlike collections.

There is also a set of actions defined for Java streams. Not only are those actions the same for any kind of stream, they also have familiar names for those that come from totally different languages. There's the `map()` function in JavaScript, which does the same as the `map()` method in Java.

The idea of making extensive use of small, reusable, and composable functions comes directly from functional programming, which we discussed in the previous chapter. They allow us to write code in a manner that tells *what* we want to do, instead of *how* we want to do it.

But in Java, to use those functions, we have to either receive a stream or create a stream from a collection.

In Java, in order to get to all this functional goodness for collections, we can do the following:

```
Arrays.asList("a", "b", "c") // Initialize list
    .stream() // Convert to stream
    .map(...) // Do something functional here
    .toList() // Convert back to list
```

In Kotlin, you can do the same:

```
listOf("a", "b", "c").stream().map{...}.toList()
```

But all those methods and more are available directly on collections:

```
listOf("a", "b", "c").map(...)
```

That's all; there is no need to convert from the stream and back unless you plan to operate on *infinite data* in the first place.

Of course, it's not as simple as that, but we cover the differences and pitfalls near the end of this chapter, in the *Streams are lazy, collections are not* section. Let's start by understanding what those weird functions actually do.

In this chapter, we won't be able to cover all the functions available on collections, but we'll cover the most widely used ones.

The examples will be somewhat boring, mostly lists of numbers, letters, and people. That's to let you focus on how each function actually works. We'll go back to some crazy examples in the next chapter. Stay tuned.

The it notation

We glanced at the notion of it briefly in previous chapters, but for this chapter, we need to understand it a bit more (pun intended).

Kotlin is all about brevity. First, if our lambda doesn't have an argument, we don't need to specify anything:

```
val noParameters = { 1 } // () -> Int implicitly
```

But what if we have a function that takes another function as an argument (and doesn't do anything with it for simplicity)? See the following code:

```
fun oneParameter(block: (Int)->Long){ }
```

We can specify both the argument name and type explicitly, and wrap them in brackets, like any other function invocation:

```
val oneParameterVeryVeryExplicit = oneParameter( {x: Int -> x.toLong() })
```

But since the lambda is the last parameter (and the only one, in this case), we can omit the brackets:

```
val oneParameterVeryExplicit = oneParameter {x: Int -> x.toLong() }
```

And since the compiler can infer the type of parameter, we can omit it too:

```
val oneParameterExplicit = oneParameter {x -> x.toLong() }
```

And since x is the only parameter, we can use the implicit name for it, which is it:

```
val oneParameterImplicit = oneParameter { it.toLong() }
```

We'll use the shortest notation in most of the following examples.

The map() function

One of the most well known higher-order functions on collections is map().

Let's say you have a function that receives a list of strings and returns a new list of the same size containing each string concatenated to itself:

```
val letters = listOf("a", "b", "c", "d")

println(repeatAll(letters)) // [aa, bb, cc, dd]
```

The task is quite trivial:

```
fun repeatAll(letters: List<String>): MutableList<String> {
    val repeatedLetters = mutableListOf<String>()

    for (l in letters) {
        repeatedLetters.add(l + l)
    }
    return repeatedLetters
}
```

But for such a trivial task, we had to write quite a lot of code. What would we have to change in order to capitalize each string instead of repeating it twice? We would like to change only this line:

```
repeatedLetters.add(l + l)  ----> repeatedLetters.add(l.toUpperCase())
```

But we have to create another function for that.

Of course, in Kotlin, we could pass a function as a second parameter. And since we don't actually care what the type is, as long as it's the same for both input and output, we can use generics:

```
fun <T> repeatSomething(input: List<T>, action: (T) -> T): MutableList<T> {
    val result = mutableListOf<T>()
    for (i in input) {
        result.add(action(i))
    }
    return result
}
```

Now we can call our *generified* function as follows:

```
println(repeatSomething(letters) {
    it.toUpperCase()
})
```

And that's almost exactly what `.map()` does:

```
println(letters.map {
    it.toUpperCase()
})
```

Another variation of `map()` is `mapTo()`.

In addition to the lambda, it receives the destination where the results should be incorporated.

You could do the following:

```
val letters = listOf("a", "B", "c", "D")
val results = mutableListOf<String>()

results.addAll(letters.map {
    it.toUpperCase()
})

results.addAll(letters.map {
```

```
        it.toLowerCase()
})

println(results)
```

But `mapTo()` lets you do this:

```
val letters = listOf("a", "B", "c", "D")
val results = mutableListOf<String>()

letters.mapTo(results) {
    it.toUpperCase()
}

letters.mapTo(results) {
    it.toLowerCase()
}

println(results)
```

In the second option, we use the results list as an argument, which allows us to reduce code nesting.

Filter family

Another common task is filtering a collection. You know the drill. You iterate over it and put only values that fit your criteria in a new collection. For example, if given a range of numbers between 1-10, we would like to return only odd ones. Of course, we've already learned this lesson from the previous example, and wouldn't simply create a function called `filterOdd()`, as later we would be required to also implement `filterEven()`, `filterPrime()`, and so on. We'll receive a lambda as the second argument right away:

```
fun filter(numbers: List<Int>, check: (Int)->Boolean): MutableList<Int> {
    val result = mutableListOf<Int>()

    for (n in numbers) {
        if (check(n)) {
            result.add(n)
        }
    }

    return result
}
```

Invoking it will print only odd numbers. How odd:

```
println(filter((1..10).toList()) {
    it % 2 != 0
}) // [1, 3, 5, 7, 9]
```

And, of course, we have a built-in function that does exactly that already:

```
println((1..10).toList().filter {
    it % 2 != 0
})
```

Find family

Say you have an unordered list of objects:

```
data class Person(val firstName: String,
                  val lastName: String,
                  val age: Int)
val people = listOf(Person("Jane", "Doe", 19),
            Person("John", "Doe", 24),
            Person("John", "Smith", 23))
```

And would like to find a first object that matches *some criteria*. Using extension functions, you could write something like this:

```
fun <T> List<T>.find(check: (T) -> Boolean): T? {
    for (p in this) {
        if (check(p)) {
            return p
        }
    }
    return null
}
```

And then, when you have a list of objects, you can simply call `find()` on it:

```
println(people.find {
    it.firstName == "John"
}) // Person(firstName=John, lastName=Doe)
```

Luckily, you don't have to implement anything. This method is already implemented for you in Kotlin.

There's also an accompanying `findLast()` method, which does the same, but which starts with the last element of the collection:

```
println(people.findLast {
    it.firstName == "John"
}) // Person(firstName=John, lastName=Smith)
```

Drop family

OK, this is cool if you have to iterate over all elements in your collection anyway. But with the `for` loops in Java, you could do something like this:

```
// Skips first two elements
for (int i = 2; i < list.size(); i++) {
    // Do something here
}
```

How are you going to achieve that with your funky functions, huh?

Well, for that there's `drop()`:

```
val numbers = (1..5).toList()
println(numbers.drop(2)) // [3, 4, 5]
```

Do note that this doesn't modify the original collection in any way:

```
println(numbers) // [1, 2, 3, 4, 5]
```

If you would like to stop your *loop* earlier, there's `dropLast()` for that:

```
println(numbers.dropLast(2)) // [1, 2, 3]
```

Another interesting function is `dropWhile()`, in which it receives a predicate instead of a number. It skips until the predicate returns true for the first time:

```
val readings = listOf(-7, -2, -1, -1, 0, 1, 3, 4)

println(readings.dropWhile {
    it <= 0
}) // [1, 3, 4]
```

And there's the accompanying `dropLastWhile()`.

Sort family

Don't worry, we won't have to implement our own sort algorithm. This is not CS 101.

Having the list of people from the preceding `find()` example, we would like to sort them by age:

```
val people = listOf(Person("Jane", "Doe", 19),
        Person("John", "Doe", 24),
        Person("John", "Smith", 23))
```

It is easily achieved with `sortedBy()`:

```
println(people.sortedBy { it.age })
```

The preceding code prints the following output:

[Person(firstName=Jane, lastName=Doe, age=19), Person(firstName=John, lastName=Smith, age=23), Person(firstName=John, lastName=Doe, age=24)]

There's also `sortedByDescending()`, which will reverse the order of the results:

```
println(people.sortedByDescending { it.lastName })
```

The preceding code prints the following output:

[Person(firstName=John, lastName=Smith, age=23), Person(firstName=John, lastName=Doe, age=24), Person(firstName=Jane, lastName=Doe, age=19)]

And if you want to compare by more than one parameter, use the combination of `sortedWith` and `compareBy`:

```
println(people.sortedWith(compareBy({it.lastName}, {it.age})))
```

ForEach

This is the first *terminator* we'll see. Terminator functions return something other than a new collection, so you can't chain the result of this call to other calls.

In the case of `forEach()`, it returns Unit. So it's like the plain, old `for` loop:

```
val numbers = (0..5)

numbers.map { it * it}        // Can continue
       .filter { it < 20 }    // Can continue
```

```
    .sortedDescending()      // Still can
    .forEach { println(it) } // Cannot continue
```

Do note that `forEach()` has some minor performance impacts compared to the traditional `for` loop.

There's also `forEachIndexed()`, which provides an index in the collection alongside the actual value:

```
numbers.map { it * it }
        .forEachIndexed { index, value ->
    print("$index:$value, ")
}
```

The output for the preceding code will be as follows:

```
0:1, 1:4, 2:9, 3:16, 4:25,
```

Since Kotlin 1.1, there's also the `onEach()` function, which is a bit more useful, since it returns the collection again:

```
numbers.map { it * it}
        .filter { it < 20 }
        .sortedDescending()
        .onEach { println(it) } // Can continue now
        .filter { it > 5 }
```

Join family

In the previous example, we used the side effect of printing to the console, which is not favorable in terms of functional programming. What's more, we also have this ugly comma at the end of our output as follows:

```
0:1, 1:4, 2:9, 3:16, 4:25,
```

There must be a better way.

How many times have you had to actually write code to simply concatenate some list of values into a string? Well, Kotlin has a function for that:

```
        val numbers = (1..5)

        println(numbers.joinToString { "$it"})
```

The preceding code will give the following output:

```
1, 2, 3, 4, 5
```

Simply beautiful, isn't it?

And if you want to separate it with other characters, or don't want spaces, there's a way to configure it:

```
println(numbers.joinToString(separator = "#") { "$it"})
```

The output of the preceding code will be as follows:

```
1#2#3#4#5
```

Fold/Reduce

Much like `forEach()`, both `fold()` and `reduce()` are terminating functions. But instead of terminating with Unit, which is not useful, they terminate with a single value of the same type.

The most common example of `reduce` is, of course, for adding up stuff. With the list of people from the previous example, we can do the following:

```
println(people.reduce {p1, p2 ->
        Person("Combined", "Age", p1.age + p2.age)
    })
```

The output of the preceding code will be as follows:

```
Person(firstName=Combined, lastName=Age, age=64)
```

Well, combining a lot of people into one doesn't make much sense, unless you're a fan of some horror movies.

But with reduce, we can also compute who's the oldest or the youngest in the list:

```
println(people.reduce {p1, p2 ->
    if (p1.age > p2.age) { p1 } else { p2 }
})
```

The second function we're about to discuss, `fold()`, is much like `reduce`, but it takes another argument, which is the initial value. It's useful when you've already computed something, and now want to use this intermediate result:

```
println(people.drop(1) // Skipping first one
        .fold(people.first()) // Using first one as initial value
            {p1, p2 ->
    Person("Combined", "Age", p1.age + p2.age)
})
```

Flat family

Say you have a list of other lists. You probably got it from different database queries, or maybe from different configuration files:

```
val listOfLists = listOf(listOf(1, 2),
        listOf(3, 4, 5), listOf(6, 7, 8))

// [[1, 2], [3, 4, 5], [6, 7, 8]]
```

And you want to turn them into a single list such as the following:

```
[1, 2, 3, 4, 5, 6, 7, 8]
```

One way to merge those lists is to write some imperative code:

```
val results = mutableListOf<Int>()

for (l in listOfLists) {
    results.addAll(l)
}
```

But calling `flatten()` will do the same for you:

```
listOfLists.flatten()
```

You can also control what happens with those results using `flatMap()`:

```
println(listOfLists.flatMap {
    it.asReversed()
})
```

Note that in this case, it refers to one of the sublists.

You can also decide to use `flatMap()` for type conversions:

```
println(listOfLists.flatMap {
    it.map { it.toDouble() }
//    ^            ^
// (1)          (2)
})
```

The preceding code prints the following output:

```
[1.0, 2.0, 3.0, 4.0, 5.0, 6.0, 7.0, 8.0]
```

We converted all integers to doubles, and then merged them into a single list.

Note how the first `it` refers to one of the lists, while the second `it` refers to a single item inside the current list.

As far as `flatten()` goes, it flattens only one level down. To demonstrate that, we'll use `Set` for the first level of nesting, `List` for the second level of nesting, and `Set` again for the third level of nesting:

```
val setOfListsOfSets = setOf(
//                        ^
//                       (1)
        listOf(setOf(1, 2), setOf(3, 4, 5), setOf(6, 7, 8)),
//          ^       ^
//         (2)     (3)
        listOf(setOf(9, 10), setOf(11, 12))
//          ^       ^
//         (2)     (3)
)
// Prints [[[1, 2], [3, 4, 5], [6, 7, 8]], [[9, 10], [11, 12]]]
```

If we call `flatten` once, we receive only the first level flattened:

```
println(setOfListsOfSets.flatten())
```

The preceding code prints the following output:

```
[[1, 2], [3, 4, 5], [6, 7, 8], [9, 10], [11, 12]]
```

To completely flatten the list, we need to call `flatten()` twice:

```
println(setOfListsOfSets.flatten().flatten())
```

The preceding code prints the following output:

```
[1, 2, 3, 4, 5, 6, 7, 8, 9, 10, 11, 12]
```

Kotlin prevents us from calling `flatten()` three times, as it recognizes the amount of nesting we have:

```
//Won't compile
println(setOfListsOfSets.flatten().flatten().flatten())
```

Slice

Say we have a list of elements, as follows:

```
val numbers = (1..10).toList()
// Prints [1, 2, 3, 4, 5, 6, 7, 8, 9, 10]
```

We can take only part of this list using `slice()`:

```
println(numbers.slice((0..3)))
// Prints [1, 2, 3, 4], last index is included
```

We're using Kotlin ranges, which is a nice syntax.

In Java, there's a `subList()` method, which is similar, but not inclusive:

```
println(numbers.subList(0, 3))
// Prints [1, 2, 3], last index is excluded
```

Chunked

It's very common to see this chunking logic in production code.

You have a huge list of identifiers that you read from somewhere and you need to check whether your database or some remote service contains them. But there are limitations on how many identifiers you can pass with a single request. Databases, for example, often have limitations of the number of arguments to a query and on the total query length:

```
fun dbCall(ids: List<Int>) {
    if (ids.size > 1000) {
        throw RuntimeException("Can't process more than 1000 ids")
    }
```

```
        // Does something here
    }
```

We can't simply pass an entire list to our function:

```
    // That will fail at runtime
    dbCall(hugeList)
```

So, we write large piles of imperative code:

```
    val pageSize = 1000
    val pages = hugeList.size / pageSize

    for (i in 0..pages) {
        val from = i * pageSize
        val p = (i+1) * pageSize
        val to = minOf(p, hugeList.size)
        dbCall(hugeList.slice(from until to))
    }
```

Luckily, since Kotlin 1.2, there's the chunked() function for that:

```
    hugeList.chunked(pageSize) {
        dbCall(it)
    }
```

Zip/Unzip

Not related to archiving in any way, zip() allows us to create pairs out of two lists based on their indexes. That may sound confusing, so let's look at an example.

We have two functions, one fetching all active employees, and the other for how many days the employee was employed in our startup:

```
    val employeeIds = listOf(5, 8, 13, 21, 34, 55, 89)
    val daysInCompany = listOf(176, 145, 117, 92, 70, 51, 35, 22, 12, 5)
```

Calling zip() between the two of them will produce the following result:

```
    println(employeeIds.zip(daysInCompany))
```

The preceding code prints the following output:

```
[(5, 176), (8, 145), (13, 117), (21, 92), (34, 70), (55, 51), (89, 35)]
```

Note that since we had a bug in our second function, and returned the days for the employees that had already left our startup, the length of the two lists wasn't equal, to begin with. Calling `zip()` will always produce the shortest list of pairs:

```
println(daysInCompany.zip(employeeIds))
```

The preceding code prints the following output:

```
[(176, 5), (145, 8), (117, 13), (92, 21), (70, 34), (51, 55), (35, 89)]
```

Note that this is not a map, but a list of pairs.

Having such a list, we can also unzip it:

```
val employeesToDays = employeeIds.zip(daysInCompany)

val (employees, days) = employeesToDays.unzip()
println(employees)
println(days)
```

The preceding code prints the following:

```
[5, 8, 13, 21, 34, 55, 89]
[176, 145, 117, 92, 70, 51, 35]
```

Streams are lazy, collections are not

Be careful with those functions on large collections, though. Most of them will copy the collection for the sake of immutability.

Functions starting with `as` won't do that, though:

```
// Returns a view, no copy here
(1..10).toList().asReversed()

// Same here
(1..10).toList().asSequence()
```

To understand the difference, check the following code:

```
val numbers = (1..1_000_000).toList()
println(measureTimeMillis {
    numbers.stream().map {
        it * it
    }
}) // ~2ms

println(measureTimeMillis {
    numbers.map {
        it * it
    }
}) // ~19ms
```

You'll notice that code using `stream()` actually never executes. Streams, being lazy, wait for a terminating function call. Functions on collections, on the other hand, execute one after the other.

If we add the terminating call though, we'll see totally different numbers:

```
println(measureTimeMillis {
    numbers.stream().map {
        it * it
    }.toList()
}) // ~70ms
```

Converting from the stream back to the list is an expensive operation. Take those points into consideration when deciding which approach to use.

Sequences

Since streams were introduced only in Java 8, but Kotlin is backward-compatible down to Java 6, it needed to provide another solution for the possibility of infinite collections. This solution was named *sequenced*, so it won't clash with Java streams when they're available.

You can generate an infinite sequence of numbers, starting with 1:

```
val seq = generateSequence(1) { it + 1 }
```

To take only the first 100, we use the `take()` function:

```
seq.take(100).forEach {
    println(it)
}
```

A finite number of sequences can be created by returning `null`:

```
val finiteSequence = generateSequence(1) {
    if (it < 1000) it + 1 else null
}

finiteSequence.forEach {
        println(it)
} // Prints numbers up to 1000
```

A finite number of sequences can be created from ranges or collections by calling `asSequence()`:

```
(1..1000).asSequence()
```

Summary

This chapter was dedicated to practicing functional programming principles and learning the building blocks of functional programming in Kotlin.

Now you should know how to transform your data with `map()`/`mapTo()`, how to `filter()` collections, and `find()` elements by criteria.

You should also be familiar with how to `drop()` elements to skip them, how to `sort()` collections, and how to iterate over them using `forEach()` and `onEach()`.

Use `join()` to stringify collections, `fold()` and `reduce()` to total collections up, and `flatten()` and `flatTo()` to reduce collection nesting.

`slice()` is a way to get only a portion of a collection, while `chunked()` is used to break a collection into even portions.

Finally, `zip()` and `unzip()` combine two collections into a pair, or split the pair back into two parts.

In the next chapter, we'll discuss how familiarity with those methods helps us to become truly reactive.

7
Staying Reactive

Once we're familiar with functional programming and its building blocks, we can start discussing reactive programming concepts. While it's not coupled with functional programming (you can be reactive while writing object-oriented or procedural code, too), it's still better to discuss after learning about functional programming and its foundation.

In this chapter, we will cover the following topics:

- Reactive principles
- Reactive extension

Reactive principles

So, what is reactive programming?

It's summarized nicely by the reactive manifesto: `https://www.reactivemanifesto.org`.

To cite it, reactive programs are:

- Responsive
- Resilient
- Elastic
- Message-driven

To understand these four topics, let's imagine 10 people standing in a line for a cashier. Each one of them can see only the person in front, but not how many people are in the line ahead of that person or what the cashier is doing. Do you have this picture in your mind? Let's start then.

Responsiveness

Would you stand in that line for the cashier?

That depends on the urgency and how much time you have. If you're in a hurry, you'll probably leave empty-handed before reaching the cash register.

That's a system being unresponsive to you. You're often in the same situation when reaching a call center of one of the service providers by phone. You're asked to wait on the line, and you wait. But, more often than not, a nice automatic voice tells you how many people are waiting on the same line ahead of you or even how much time you'll have to wait.

In both cases, the result is the same. You've wasted your time waiting in line or on the line. But the second system was responsive to your needs, and you could make decisions based on that.

Resiliency

Let's continue to resiliency. You're waiting on the line for 10 minutes, then the line drops. Or, you reached one of the customer care representatives, but they hang up on you by mistake. How often does that happen? That's the system not being resilient to failures. Or, you've waited in line for half an hour to see a doctor, when they suddenly leave the office and go to a golf club, asking you to come back tomorrow. That's a system that wasn't responsive in the face of failure.

The reactive manifesto discusses various ways to achieve resiliency:

- Delegation
- Replication
- Containment
- Isolation

Delegation is when the doctor comes out of their office and tells you, *I can't see you today, but knock on the other door; they'll see to you soon.*

Replication is for a clinic to always have two doctors available, just in the event that one of them miss their favorite team playing this evening. It relates to elasticity, which we'll discuss in the next section.

Containment and isolation are usually discussed together. What if you actually don't need to see the doctor? Maybe you only need a prescription from them. Then, you could leave them a message (we'll discuss message-passing soon, as it's also an important part of reactiveness) and they'll send you a recipe when they're between games. You decoupled yourself from seeing a doctor. It also provided you with isolation from the doctors' failures or problems. What you didn't know is that, while printing your recipe, their computer crashed twice and they were really stressed about that. But because you weren't in front of them, they kept that to themselves.

Elasticity

So, in the previous section, we discussed replication. To prevent failures, our clinic always has two doctors available. Maybe the second doctor served some patients, or maybe they were just patiently waiting for the first doctor to leave for their football game to start working.

But, what would happen to that resilient system if suddenly there is a flu epidemic or a band of rabid squirrels starts attacking citizens in the nearby park? Two doctors won't be able to handle all of the patients and then, again, we have a problem with resiliency.

But what if we had a supply of retired doctors sitting in their homes playing mahjong? Certainly, we could call them to come and help bandage all of those squirrel victims. And after they were all properly treated, the doctors could return to their mahjong.

That's a system being elastic depending on the workload.

Elasticity builds on scalability. We could treat all of those patients because each doctor could work independently. But what if all of the bandages were stored in a single box? Then it would create a bottleneck, with all of those doctors standing around waiting for the next pack of bandages.

Message-driven

This is also referred to as *asynchronous message passing*. So, we saw in the *Resiliency* section that if you could leave a message for the doctor, it may make the system more resilient.

What if all of the patients would only leave messages? Then each doctor could prioritize them or batch-process those messages. For example, printing all recipes together, instead of switching between different tasks.

In addition to loose coupling and isolation, there's also *location transparency*. You didn't know tha your doctor sent you this prescription while driving home (they snuck out of the window while you left your message). But you don't care since you got what you wanted.

Using messages also allows an interesting option of *backpressure*. If your doctor receives too many messages, they may collapse from stress. To avoid that, they may text you to say that you'll have to wait a bit longer to receive your prescription. Or, if they have a secretary, we may even ask them to do that anyway. Again, we're talking about delegation here, as all of those principles are correlated.

Messages are also non-blocking. After you leave the message, you don't sit there waiting for the doctor's response. You usually go back home, to your regular tasks. The ability to perform other tasks while you wait is one of the cornerstones of concurrency.

Reactive extension

The rest of this chapter will be dedicated to the specific implementation of reactive principles in Kotlin. The predominant library in this field is RxJava. Since Kotlin is fully interoperable with Java libraries, RxKotlin is only a thin wrapper over the original RxJava. Hence, we'll discuss it as if these are one and the same library, and highlight the differences, if any.

As soon as we start talking about RxJava, you'll recognize it's built upon the **Observer** design pattern we discussed in `Chapter 4`, *Getting Familiar with Behavioral Patterns*.

We'll start by adding the following dependency to our Gradle project:

```
compile "io.reactivex.rxjava2:rxjava:2.1.14"
```

Currently, this is the latest version of RxJava2, but when you read this chapter, there will probably ba a more recent version already. Feel free to use it.

You may remember that the pattern consists of two objects:

- `publisher`: Produces data
- `subscriber`: Consumes data

In RxJava, publishers are called `Observable`.

The following code will create our first publisher:

```
val publisher = Observable.fromArray(5, 6, 7)
```

To start consuming those numbers, we can supply a lambda to the `subscribe()` function:

```
publisher.subscribe {
    println(it)
} // Prints 1, 2, 3
```

There are other functions available on `Observable` that you'll immediately recognize: `map()` and `filter()`, for example. Those are the same functions that are available on regular arrays in Kotlin:

```
publisher.filter {
    it > 5
}.map {
    it + it
}.subscribe {
    println(it)
}
```

OK, this is nice, but we've already discussed collections and streams in sequences in the previous chapter. Why do it again?

Let's look at the following example:

```
val publisher = Observable.interval(1, TimeUnit.SECONDS)

publisher.subscribe {
    println("P1 $it")
}

publisher.subscribe {
    println("P2 $it")
}

Thread.sleep(TimeUnit.SECONDS.toMillis(5))
```

This code will wait for five milliseconds before terminating and it will print the following:

```
Sleeping <= This was the last line in our code, actually
P2 0    <= P2 came after P1 in code, but it comes before now
P1 0
P2 1
P1 1
P2 2
P1 2
```

This is unexpected. `Sleeping` was the last line in the code, but it's printed first. Then notice that `P2` is printed before `P1` sometimes if you run this example more than once. And sometimes, it's `P1` before `P2`, much like in the code. What's going on here?

That's asynchronicity in action. We need `Thread.sleep()` here to allow our listeners to run for some time, otherwise, our program would terminate. And when they're called, it doesn't matter where in the actual code they were placed.

 In this chapter, we'll use `Thread.sleep()` and `CountDownLatch` a lot to demonstrate how asynchronism works. In a real-life application, you should never use `Thread.sleep`. If you're still not familiar with `CountDownLatch`, don't worry, we'll explain how it works the first time we stumble upon it, in the *Flowables* section.

Well, that's how the Observer design pattern behaves, naturally. But with Observer, there's also an option to unsubscribe. How do we achieve it here?

Let's replace the second listener with the following code:

```
...
val subscription = publisher.subscribe {
    println("P2 $it")
}

println("Sleeping")
Thread.sleep(TimeUnit.SECONDS.toMillis(2))
subscription.dispose()
...
```

A call to `subscribe()` returns a `Disposable`. When you no longer want to receive updates, you can call `dispose()` on it, which is synonymous with *unsubscribe*.

Your output may look like this:

```
Sleeping
P1 0        <= Notice that P1 is the first one now
P2 0
P1 1
Sleeping    <= This is after dispose/unsubscribe
P2 1        <= But it may still take some time, so P2 prints again
P1 2
P1 3
P1 4        <= No more prints from P2, it unsubscribed
```

What if we were to create our own `Observable`, with its own specific logic? There's a `create()` method for that:

```
val o = Observable.create<Int> {
    for (i in 1..10_000) {
        it.onNext(i)
    }
    it.onComplete()
}
```

We create an `Observable` that publishes numbers. To push a new value to all listeners, we use the `onNext()` method. We notify the listeners that there's no more data with `onComplete()`. Finally, if an error occurrs, we can call `onError()`, supplying the exception as an argument.

You'll notice that if we try to actually call `onError()`, we'll get an exception:

```
val o = Observable.create<Int> {
    it.onError(RuntimeException())
}

o.subscribe {
    println("All went good: $it")
} // OnErrorNotImplementedException
```

That's because we use the shorthand form with the lambda listener.

If we want to handle errors correctly, we also need to supply *error handler* as a second argument:

```
o.subscribe({
    println("All went good: $it")
}, {
    println("There was an error $it")
})
```

There's also a third parameter, which is the `onComplete` handler:

```
o.subscribe({
    println("All went good: $it")
}, {
    println("There was an error $it")
}, {
    println("Publisher closed the stream")
})
```

In our examples, we'll rarely use error handlers since our code is very basic. But you should always provide them in real applications.

Hot Observable

Hot `Observable` is a term we'll use a lot in this chapter, as opposed to cold `Observable`. All Observable we discussed before was cold. That meant they knew everything that happened from the beginning of time, and each time somebody asked them politely, they could repeat the whole history. Hot `Observable` only know what happens now. Think of the weather forecast and weather history, for example. The weather forecast is hot—you'll get the current weather, let's say every minute. The weather history is cold–you can get the whole history of weather changes, if you care about it. If you still don't get this concept, don't worry too much. We have half of the chapter ahead of us to cover it.

As you've probably noticed, up until now, all of our subscribers always got all the data, no matter when they subscribed:

```
publisher.subscribe {
    println("S1 $it")
} // Prints 10K times

publisher.subscribe {
    println("S2 $it")
} // Also prints 10K times
```

But that's not always the case. More often, we have the data source coming from outside and not created each time by the `publisher`:

```
val iterator = (1..10).iterator()

val publisher = Observable.create<Int> {
    while (iterator.hasNext()) {
        val nextNumber = iterator.next()
        it.onNext(nextNumber)
    }
}
```

Here, instead of creating the list inside, we have a reference to its iterator.

Let's see how the following code behaves now:

```
publisher.subscribeOn(Schedulers.newThread()).subscribe {
    println("S1: $it")
    Thread.sleep(10)
}

Thread.sleep(50)

publisher.subscribeOn(Schedulers.newThread()).subscribe {
    println("S2: $it")
    Thread.sleep(10)
}

Thread.sleep(50)
```

We have two subscribers, as before. Up until now, all subscribers executed on the same thread we were running. For this example, we assigned them a separate thread each. That would allow us to simulate operations that are running for some time: 10 ms, in this case. To specify on which thread subscriber should run, we use `subscribeOn()`. `Schedulers` is an utility class, much like `Executors` from Java 5. In this case, it will assign a new thread for each listener.

The output may look something like this:

```
S1: 1
S1: 2
S1: 3
S1: 4
S1: 5
S2: 6 <= That's where "Subscriber 2" begins listening
S1: 7
S2: 8
S1: 9
S2: 10
```

Notice that if every consumer received all the data previously, now the second subscriber will never receive numbers 1-5.

After the second subscriber is connected, only one of them will receive the data each time.

What if we want to publish data to all of the subscribers simultaneously?

Multicast

There's a `publish()` method for that:

```
val iterator = (1..5).iterator()
val subject = Observable.create<Int> {
    while (iterator.hasNext()) {
        val number = iterator.nextInt()
        println("P: $number")
        it.onNext(number)
        Thread.sleep(10)
    }
}.observeOn(Schedulers.newThread()).publish()
```

We again create a somewhat *hot* `Observable`, but this time we specify that it will run on a separate thread with `observeOn()`. We also use the `publish()` method, which turns our `Observable` into `ConnectableObservable`.

If we simply subscribe to this type of `Observable`, nothing will happen. We need to tell it when to start running. We use that with the `connect()` method. Since the `connect()` method is blocking, we'll execute it from a separate thread for this example:

```
thread { // Connect is blocking, so we run in on another thread
    subject.connect() // Tells observer when to start
}
```

Now we'll let publisher work for a few milliseconds, then connect our first listener:

```
Thread.sleep(10)
println("S1 Subscribes")
subject.subscribeOn(Schedulers.newThread()).subscribe {
    println("S1: $it")
    Thread.sleep(100)
}
```

After some more time, we connect a second listener, and allow them to finish:

```
Thread.sleep(20)

println("S2 Subscribes")
subject.subscribeOn(Schedulers.newThread()).subscribe {
    println("S2: $it")
    Thread.sleep(100)
}
Thread.sleep(2000)
```

Let's see the output now, as it's quite interesting:

```
P: 1 <= Publisher starts publishing even before someone subscribes
S1 Subscribes
P: 2
P: 3
S1: 3 <= Subscriber actually missed some values
S2 Subscribes
P: 4
P: 5
P: 6 <= Publisher completes here
S1: 4
S2: 4
S1: 5
S2: 5 <= Both subscribers receive same values
```

Of course, having this `connect()` is not always comfortable.

For that reason, we have a method called `refCount()`, which turns our `ConnectableObservable` back into a regular `Observable`. It will keep a reference count of the subscribers, and dispose of the subscriptions only after all subscribers have done so, too:

```
// This is a connectable Observable
val connectableSource = Observable.fromIterable((1..3)).publish()

// Should call connect() on it
dataSource.connect()

// This is regular Observable which wraps ConnectableObservable
val regularSource = connectableSource.refCount()

regularSource.connect() // Doesn't compile
```

And if calling `publish().refCount()` is too cumbersome, there's also the `share()` method that does exactly that:

```
val regularSource = Observable.fromIterable((1..3)).publish().refCount()

val stillRegular = Observable.fromIterable((1..3)).share()
```

Subject

The easiest way to understand `Subject` is that `Subject = Observable + Observer`.

On the one hand, it allows others to `subscribe()` to it. On the other, it can `subscribe` to other `Observable`:

```
val dataSource = Observable.fromIterable((1..3))

val multicast = PublishSubject.create<Int>()

multicast.subscribe {
    println("S1 $it")
}

multicast.subscribe {
    println("S2 $it")
}

dataSource.subscribe(multicast)

Thread.sleep(1000)
```

The following code prints six lines, three for each subscriber:

```
S1 1
S2 1
S1 2
S2 2
S1 3
S2 3
```

Note that we didn't use `publish()` on our `dataSource`, so it's cold. Cold means that each time somebody subscribes to this source, it will begin sending data anew. The hot `Observable`, on the other hand, doesn't have all the data, and will only send what it has from this moment on.

For that reason, we need to first connect all the listeners, and only then begin to listen to the `dataSource`.

If we're using a hot `dataSource`, we can switch the calls:

```
val dataSource = Observable.fromIterable((1..3)).publish()

val multicast = PublishSubject.create<Int>()
```

```
dataSource.subscribe(multicast)

multicast.subscribe {
    println("S1 $it")
}
println("S1 subscribed")

multicast.subscribe {
    println("S2 $it")
}
println("S2 subscribed")

dataSource.connect()

Thread.sleep(1000)
```

As in the previous section, we use `connect()` to tell `dataSource` when to start emitting data.

ReplaySubject

In addition to `PublishSubject`, which we discussed in the previous section, there are other subjects available. To understand how `ReplaySubject` works, let's see first the following example with `PublishSubject`:

```
val list = (8..23).toList() // Some non trivial numbers
val iterator = list.iterator()
val o = Observable.intervalRange(0, list.size.toLong(), 0, 10,
TimeUnit.MILLISECONDS).map {
    iterator.next()
}.publish()

val subject = PublishSubject.create<Int>()

o.subscribe(subject)

o.connect() // Start publishing

Thread.sleep(20)

println("S1 subscribes")
    subject.subscribe {
        println("S1 $it")
    }
    println("S1 subscribed")
```

```
Thread.sleep(10)

println("S2 subscribes")
subject.subscribe {
    println("S2 $it")
}
println("S2 subscribed")

Thread.sleep(1000)
```

This prints the following:

```
S1 11 <= Lost 8, 9, 10
S1 12
S2 12 <= Lost also 11
S1 13
S2 13
. . .
```

Clearly, some events are lost for good.

Now, let's replace `PublishSubject` with `ReplaySubject` and examine the output:

```
val subject = ReplaySubject.create<Int>()
```

The following output will be printed:

```
S1 subscribes
S1 8
S1 9
S1 10 <= S1 catchup
S1 subscribed
S1 11
S1 12
S2 subscribes
S2 8
S2 9
S2 10
S2 11
S2 12 <= S2 catchup
S2 subscribed
S1 13 <= Regular multicast from here
S2 13
. . .
```

With `ReplaySubject`, no events are lost. You can see from the output, though, that until some point, events aren't multicast, even when there is more than one `subscriber`. Instead, for each `subscriber`, `ReplaySubject` performs a kind of catch-up of what it missed until now.

The benefits of this approach are clear. We converted what seems to be a *hot* `Observable` into something quite *cold*. But there are also limitations. By using `ReplaySubject.create`, we produce an unbounded subject. If it tries to record too many events, we will simply run out of memory. To avoid that, we can use the `createWithSize()` method:

```
val subject = ReplaySubject.createWithSize<Int>(2)
```

It creates the following output:

```
S1 subscribes
S1 9 <= lost 8
S1 10
S1 subscribed
S1 11
S2 subscribes
S1 12
S2 11 <= lost 8, 9, 10
S2 12
S2 subscribed
S1 13
S2 13
...
```

As you can see, now our subject remembers fewer items, so the earliest events are lost.

BehaviorSubject

Imagine a situation when you have a stream of updates every minute. You want to display the latest value you received, then keep updating it when new data comes in. You can use `ReplaySubject` with a size of one. But there's also `BehaviorSubject` exactly for this case:

```
val subject = BehaviorSubject.create<Int>()
```

The output will be as follows:

```
S1 subscribes
S1 10 <= This was the most recent value, 8 and 9 are lost
S1 subscribed
S1 11 <= First update
```

```
S2 subscribes
S2 11 <= This was most recent value, 8, 9 and 10 lost
S2 subscribed
S1 12 <= As usual from here
S2 12
```

AsyncSubject

This is a strange `subject` since, unlike the others, it doesn't update its subscribers. So, what is it good for?

What if you wanted to have a very basic functionality, simply updating a screen with the latest value and never refreshing it again until the screen is closed:

```
val subject = AsyncSubject.create<Int>()
```

Here is the output:

```
S1 subscribes
S1 subscribed
S2 subscribes
S2 subscribed
S1 23 <= This is the final value
S2 23
```

Be careful, though. Since `AsyncSubject` waits for the sequence to complete, if the sequence is infinite, it will never call its subscribers:

```
// Infinite sequence of 1
val o = Observable.generate<Int> { 1 }.publish()
...
o.connect() // Hangs here forever
```

SerializedSubject

It's important not to call the `onNext()`/`onComplete()`/`onError()` methods from different threads, as it will make the calls non-serializable.

This is a **Proxy** of sorts around any regular `subject`, which synchronizes calls to the unsafe methods. You can wrap any `subject` with `SerializedSubject` using the `toSerialized()` method:

```
val subject = ReplaySubject.createWithSize<Int>(2).toSerialized()
```

Flowables

In all previous examples, we emitted data using `Observable` or `subject`, which also extends `Observable`, and it worked out pretty well.

But our listeners weren't doing much. What if they were to do something more substantial?

Let's see the following example. We'll produce a lot of unique strings:

```
val source = Observable.create<String> {
    var startProducing = System.currentTimeMillis()
    for (i in 1..10_000_000) {
        it.onNext(UUID.randomUUID().toString())

        if (i % 100_000 == 0) {
            println("Produced $i events in ${System.currentTimeMillis() -
startProducing}ms")
            startProducing = System.currentTimeMillis()
        }
    }
    latch.countDown()
}
```

We're using `CountDownLatch` so the main thread will be able to wait until we finish. In addition, we're also printing how much time it took to emit 100,000 events. This will be useful later.

In the `subscribe()` method, we would repeat those strings 1,000 times:

```
val counter = AtomicInteger(0)
source.observeOn(Schedulers.newThread())
        .subscribe( {
            it.repeat(500)
            if (counter.incrementAndGet() % 100_000 == 0) {
                println("Consumed ${counter.get()} events")
            }
        }, {
            println(it)
        })
```

`AtomicInteger` is used to count the number of processed events in a thread-safe way.

We're obviously consuming more slowly than we're producing:

```
Produced 100000 events in 1116ms
Produced 200000 events in 595ms
Produced 300000 events in 734ms
```

```
Consumed 100000 events
Produced 400000 events in 815ms
Produced 500000 events in 705ms
Consumed 200000 events
Produced 600000 events in 537ms
Produced 700000 events in 390ms
Produced 800000 events in 529ms
Produced 900000 events in 387ms
Consumed 300000 events
Produced 1000000 events in 531ms
Produced 1100000 events in 537ms
Produced 1200000 events in 11241ms <= What happens here?
Consumed 400000 events
Produced 1300000 events in 19472ms
Produced 1400000 events in 31993ms
Produced 1500000 events in 52650ms
```

But the interesting point is that, after some period, the producing time will increase dramatically.

That's the point when we start to run out of memory. Let's now replace our `Observable` with `Flowable`:

```
val source = Flowable.create<String> ({
    var startProducing = System.currentTimeMillis()
    for (i in 1..10_000_000) {
        it.onNext(UUID.randomUUID().toString())

        if (i % 100_000 == 0) {
            println("Produced $i events in ${System.currentTimeMillis() -
startProducing}ms")
            startProducing = System.currentTimeMillis()
        }
    }
    it.onComplete()
    latch.countDown()
}, BackpressureStrategy.DROP)
```

As you can see, instead of passing only a lambda, we also pass a second argument, which is `BackpressureStrategy`. What happens is that, behind the scenes, `Flowable` has a bounded buffer. This is very similar to how we could make `ReplaySubject` bounded. The second argument is telling `Flowable` what should happen if this buffer limit is reached. In this case, we're asking it to throw away those events.

Now, we should check the final part of our output:

```
...
Produced 9500000 events in 375ms
Produced 9600000 events in 344ms
Produced 9700000 events in 344ms
Consumed 2800000 events
Produced 9800000 events in 351ms
Produced 9900000 events in 333ms
Produced 10000000 events in 340ms
```

First, note that we didn't get stuck at any point. Actually, the pace of our production is constant.

Second, you should note that although we *produced* 10,000,000 events, we *consumed* only 2.8 million. All other events were dropped.

But we didn't run out of memory, which is the great benefit of `Flowable`.

If you do want `Flowable` to behave like `Observable`, you can specify `BackpressureStrategy.BUFFER`, and see that it begins to stutter around the same lines.

As a general guideline, use `Flowable` when as follows:

- You plan to emit more than 1,000 items (some may say 10,000)
- You're reading a file
- You're querying a database
- You have some network streaming to do

Use `Observable` as follows:

- You have a limited amount of data you plan to emit.
- You deal with user input. Humans aren't as quick as they think they are and don't produce many events.
- You care about the performance of the flow: `Observable` are simpler, thus faster.

When we used the lambda expression, we didn't notice much difference between `Flowable` and `Observable`.

Instead, now we'll replace it with an anonymous class and see what benefits this approach provides:

```
source.observeOn(Schedulers.newThread())
        .subscribe(object : Subscriber<String> {
    lateinit var subscription: Subscription

    override fun onSubscribe(s: Subscription?) {
        s?.let {
            this.subscription = it
        } ?: throw RuntimeException()
    }

    override fun onNext(t: String?) {
        ...
    }

    override fun onError(t: Throwable?) {
        ...
    }

    override fun onComplete() {
        ...
    }
})
```

That's obviously a lot more code. We need to implement four methods now.

What interests us the most is the `onSubscribe()` method. Here, we receive a new object called `Subscription` and store it in a property.

For now, we'll drop the fancy code that we were using in our listener before, and simply print every new string we receive:

```
override fun onNext(t: String?) {
    println(t)
}
```

Huh? That's strange. Our listener doesn't print anything.

Let's go to our `onSubscribe` and modify it a bit:

```
override fun onSubscribe(s: Subscription) {
    this.subscription = s
    this.subscription.request(100)
}
```

`Subscription` has a method called `request()`, which receives the number of items we're willing to take.

You can run the code again to see that now our subscriber prints the first 100 strings, then goes silent again.

We've already discussed the `BackpressureStrategy.DROP` and `BackpressureStrategy.BUFFER` strategies. Let's now focus on the `BackpressureStrategy.MISSING` strategy. The name is a bit confusing; *custom* would be better. We'll see why in a moment:

```
val source = Flowable.create<String> ({
    ...
}, BackpressureStrategy.MISSING)
```

And we'll go back to `onNext()`, which actually does something:

```
override fun onNext(t: String) {
    t.repeat(500) // Do something

    println(counter.get()) // Print index of this item
    this.subscription.request(1) // Request next

    if (counter.incrementAndGet() % 100_000 == 0) {
        println("Consumed ${counter.get()} events")
    }
}
```

So, we're back to repeating strings. And after we finish with each, we ask our `Flowable` to provide the next one with `subscription.request(1)`.

Quickly enough, though, we receive `MissingBackpressureException`.

That's because we specified the `BackpressureStrategy.MISSING` strategy, and didn't specify the size of the buffer.

To fix that, we'll use the `onBackpressureBuffer()` method:

```
val source = Flowable.create<String> ({
    ...
}, BackpressureStrategy.MISSING).onBackpressureBuffer(10_000)
```

That postponed the problem, but we still crash with `MissingBackpressureException`.

What we need in this case is not to *create* a `Flowable`, but to *generate* it:

```
val count = AtomicInteger(0)
// This is not entirely correct, but simplifies our code
val startTime = System.currentTimeMillis()
val source = Flowable.generate<String> {
        it.onNext(UUID.randomUUID().toString())

        if (count.incrementAndGet() == 10_000_000) {
            it.onComplete()
            latch.countDown()
        }

        if (count.get() % 100_000 == 0) {
            println("Produced ${count.get()} events in
${System.currentTimeMillis() - startTime}ms")
            startTime = System.currentTimeMillis()
        }
    }
```

Note that, unlike `create()`, `generate()` receives a lambda that represents *a single action*. For that reason, we cannot have loops inside it. Instead, we store our state, if any, outside.

The output looks as follows:

```
Produced 100000 events in 3650ms
Produced 200000 events in 1942ms
Produced 300000 events in 1583ms
Produced 400000 events in 1630ms
...
```

Take note of how much slower the production is now. That's because we wait for our consumer to process the event before supplying the next batch.

Holding state

Having those values captured in a closure may seem a bit ugly. There's a more functional alternative, but it's quite hard to grasp. Generate can receive two functions instead of one:

```
<T, S> Flowable<T> generate(Callable<S> initialState, BiFunction<S,
Emitter<T>, S> generator)
```

Well, that's a mouthful. Let's try to understand what's going on there.

The first initial state is `() -> State`. In our case, the state can be represented as follows:

```
data class State(val count: Int, val startTime: Long)
```

We don't pass an instance of `CountDownLatch` to our function for the sake of simplicity. You'll soon understand why.

So, our first argument is the `() -> State` function, which has no parameters and returns a `State`. Now, the second argument should be a function, that is, `(State, Emitter<T>) -> State`. In our case, we emit strings, so our function is `(State, Emitter<String>) -> State`.

Since this is all a bit confusing not only to us but also to the Kotlin compiler, we specify exactly what types of functions those are, `Callable<State>` and `BiFunction<State, Emitter<String>, State>`:

```
val source = Flowable.generate<String, State>(
    Callable<State> { State(0, System.currentTimeMillis()) },
    BiFunction<State, Emitter<String>, State> { state, emitter ->
        emitter.onNext(UUID.randomUUID().toString())

        // In other cases you could use destructuring
        val count = state.count + 1
        var startTime = state.startTime
        if (count == 10_000_000) {
            emitter.onComplete()
            latch.countDown()
        }

        if (count % 100_000 == 0) {
            println("Produced ${count} events in
${System.currentTimeMillis() - startTime}ms")
            startTime = System.currentTimeMillis()
        }
        // Return next state
        State(count, startTime)
    }
)
```

As you can see, sometimes purely functional code is much more complex. Luckily for us, Kotlin allows us to chose different approaches for different situations.

FlowableProcessor

Much like any `Subject` is an `Observer` and `Observable` at the same time, any `FlowableProcessor` is a `Flowable` that is both a `Publisher` and `Subscriber`.

To understand this statement, let's take the example of `ReplaySubject` and rewrite it using `ReplayProcessor`:

```
val list = (8..23).toList() // Some non trivial numbers
val iterator = list.iterator()
val o = Observable.intervalRange(0, list.size.toLong(), 0, 10,
TimeUnit.MILLISECONDS).map {
    iterator.next()
}.toFlowable(BackpressureStrategy.DROP).publish()
```

Any `Observable` can be converted to `Flowable` using the `toFlowable()` method. As with any `Flowable`, we need to specify which strategy to use. In our case, we use `BackpressureStrategy.DROP`.

As you can see, `Flowable` supports the `publish()` method, the same as `Observable`:

```
val processor = ReplayProcessor.createWithSize<Int>(2)
```

Instead of creating `ReplaySubject`, we create `ReplayProcessor`, which also supports size limiting:

```
o.subscribe(processor)

o.connect() // Start publishing

Thread.sleep(20)

println("S1 subscribes")
processor.subscribe {
    println("S1 $it")
}
println("S1 subscribed")

Thread.sleep(10)

println("S2 subscribes")
processor.subscribe {
    println("S2 $it")
}
println("S2 subscribed")
```

```
Thread.sleep(1000)
```

The output is practically the same:

```
S1 subscribes
S1 9
S1 10
S1 subscribed
S1 11
S2 subscribes
S2 10
S2 11
S2 subscribed
S1 12
S2 12
```

But in case of big input, we now have backpressure to protect us.

Batching

Sometimes, slowing the producer is not possible. So, are we back to the original problem, of either dropping some events or running out of memory? Luckily, Rx still has a few tricks up its sleeve. It is often more efficient to process data in batches. We've already discussed such a case in the previous chapter. For that, we can specify `buffer()` for our `subseriber`.

Buffer has three flavors. The first one is batch-per-size:

```
val latch = CountDownLatch(1)
val o = Observable.intervalRange(8L, 15L, 0L, 100L, TimeUnit.MILLISECONDS)

o.buffer(3).subscribe({
    println(it)
}, {}, { latch.countDown()})

latch.await()
```

It outputs the following:

```
[8, 9, 10]
[11, 12, 13]
[14, 15, 16]
[17, 18, 19]
[20, 21, 22]
```

The second is the batch-per-time interval. Imagine we have a screen with a screen that displays the latest news, and new updates arrive every few seconds. But for us, it's fine to refresh the view only once every five seconds:

```
val latch = CountDownLatch(1)
val o = Observable.intervalRange(8L, 15L, 0L, 100L, TimeUnit.MILLISECONDS)

o.buffer(300L, TimeUnit.MILLISECONDS).subscribe ({
    println(it)
}, {}, { latch.countDown() })

latch.await()
```

It outputs the following:

```
[8, 9, 10, 11]
[12, 13, 14]
[15, 16, 17]
[18, 19, 20]
[21, 22]
```

The third flavor allows us to become dependent on another `Observable`. We'll batch until it asks us to flush the data:

```
val latch = CountDownLatch(1)
val o = Observable.intervalRange(8L, 15L, 0L, 100L, TimeUnit.MILLISECONDS)

o.buffer(Observable.interval(200L, TimeUnit.MILLISECONDS)).subscribe ({
    println(it)
}, {}, { latch.countDown() })

latch.await()
```

It outputs the following:

```
[8, 9, 10]
[11, 12]
[13, 14]
[15, 16]
[17, 18]
[19, 20]
[21, 22]
[]
```

Throttling

Throttling on the consumer side is similar to dropping on the producer side. But it can be applied not only to `Flowable`, but also to `Observable`.

You specify the time interval, and each time get only one element, either the first or last one, in that interval:

```
val o = PublishSubject.intervalRange(8L, 15L, 0L, 100L,
TimeUnit.MILLISECONDS).publish()

o.throttleFirst(280L, TimeUnit.MILLISECONDS).subscribe {
    println(it)
}

o.buffer(280L, TimeUnit.MILLISECONDS).subscribe {
    println(it)
}

o.connect()

Thread.sleep(100 * 15)
```

Execute this example a few times and you will see that you get different results. Throttling is highly sensitive to timing.

`throttleFirst()` outputs `[8, 11, 15, 17, 21]` because it received the following windows:

```
8
[8, 9, 10]
11
[11, 12, 13]
14
[14, 15, 16]
17
[17, 18, 19]
20
[20, 21]
[22]
```

Notice that `[22]` is throttled and never printed.

Now, let's see what happens when we use `throttleLast()`, instead:

```
val o = Observable.intervalRange(8L, 15L, 5L, 100L, TimeUnit.MILLISECONDS)

o.throttleLast(280L, TimeUnit.MILLISECONDS).subscribe {
    println(it)
}

o.buffer(280L,  TimeUnit.MILLISECONDS).subscribe {
    println(it)
}

Thread.sleep(100 * 30)
```

`throttleLast()` outputs `[10, 13, 16, 19, 22]` because it received the following windows:

```
10
[8, 9, 10]
13
[11, 12, 13]
16
[14, 15, 16]
19
[17, 18, 19]
21
[20, 21]
[22]
```

Again, `[22]` is throttled and never printed.

Throttling is the last resiliency tool we'll discuss in this chapter, but it's probably one of the most useful ones.

Summary

In this chapter, we learned about the main benefits of reactive systems. Such systems should be responsive, resilient, elastic, and driven by messaging.

We also discussed the Java 9 Reactive Streams API and its most popular implementation, which is Rx.

Now you should better understand the difference between cold and hot `Observable`. A cold `Observable` starts working only when someone subscribes to it. A hot `Observable`, on the other hand, always emits events, even if nobody is listening.

We also discussed the concept of backpressure, implemented with `Flowable`. It allows for a feedback mechanism between the producer and consumer.

In addition, you should be familiar with the notion of multicasting using subjects. It allows us to send the same message to multiple listeners.

Finally, we discussed some resilience mechanisms, such as buffering and throttling, that allow us to accumulate or drop messages, in case we're unable to process them in time.

In the next chapter, we'll start discussing threads, a concept that should be familiar to you if you come from a Java background, and coroutines, which are lightweight threads introduced in Kotlin 1.1.

8
Threads and Coroutines

In this chapter, we'll discuss how our application can efficiently serve thousands of requests per second. In the previous chapter, we already had one glimpse at it—**reactive streams** use a number of different threads (exposed by the `Schedulers` API), and we even had to create a thread once or twice with the `thread()` function. But before we dive into nuances, let's first discuss what kind of problems threads are able to solve.

In your laptop, you have a CPU with multiple cores, probably four of them. That means that it can do four different computations *in parallel*, which is pretty amazing, considering that 10 years ago, a single-core CPU was the default and even two cores were only for enthusiasts.

But even back then, you were not actually limited to doing only a single task at a time, right? You could listen to music and browse the internet at the same time, even on a single-core CPU. How does your CPU manage to pull that off? Well, the same way your brain does. It juggles tasks. When you're reading a book while listening to your friend talking, part of the time you're not really reading and part of the time you're not really listening. That is until we get at least two cores in our brains.

The servers you run your code on have pretty much the same CPU. Which still means they can serve four requests simultaneously. But what if you have 10,000 requests per second? You can't serve them in parallel, because you don't have 10,000 CPU cores. But you can try and serve them concurrently.

In this chapter, we will cover the following topics:

- Threads
- Coroutines
- Channels

Threads

The most basic concurrency model is provided by JVM threads. Threads allow us to run code concurrently (but not necessarily in parallel), making better use of multiple CPU cores, for example. They are more lightweight than processes. One process may spawn hundreds of threads. Unlike processes, sharing data between threads is easy. But that also introduces a lot of problems, as we'll see later.

Let's see how we create two threads in Java first:

```java
new Thread(() -> {
    for (int i = 0; i < 100; i++) {
        System.out.println("T1: " + i);
    }
}).start();

new Thread(() -> {
    for (int i = 0; i < 100; i++) {
        System.out.println("T2: " + i);
    }
}).start();
```

The output will look something like this:

```
...
T2: 12
T2: 13
T1: 60
T2: 14
T1: 61
T2: 15
T2: 16
...
```

Note that the output will vary between executions, and at no point is it guaranteed to be interleaved.

The same code in Kotlin would look as follows:

```kotlin
val t1 = thread {
    for (i in 1..100) {
        println("T1: $i")
    }
}

val t2 = thread {
    for (i in 1..100) {
```

```
        println("T2: $i")
    }
}
```

In Kotlin, there's less boilerplate, because there's a function that helps us create a new thread. Notice that unlike Java, we don't need to call `start()` to launch the thread. It starts by default. If we would like to postpone it for later, we can set the `start` parameter to `false`:

```
val t2 = thread(start = false) {
    for (i in 1..100) {
        println("T2: $i")
    }
}
...
// Later
t2.start()
```

Another useful concept from Java is *daemon threads*. These threads don't prevent JVM from exiting and are very good for non-critical background tasks.

In Java, the API is not fluent, so we'll have to assign our thread to a variable, set it to be a daemon thread, and then start it:

```
Thread t1 = new Thread(() -> {
    for (int i = 0; i < 100; i++) {
        System.out.println("T1: " + i);
    }
});
t1.setDaemon(true);
t1.start();
```

In Kotlin, this is much simpler:

```
val t3 = thread(isDaemon = true) {
    for (i in 1..1_000_000) {
        println("T3: $i")
    }
}
```

Notice that although we asked this thread to print numbers up to one million, it prints only a few hundred. That's because it's a daemon thread. When the parent thread stops, it stops too.

Thread safety

There are many books written about thread safety and there are good reasons for that. Concurrency bugs that are caused by lack of thread safety are the ones hardest to track. They're hard to reproduce, because you'll usually need a lot of threads competing on the same resource for an actual race to happen. Because this book is about Kotlin and not thread safety in general, we'll only scratch the surface of this topic. If you're interested in the topic of thread safety in the JVM language, you should check out the book *Java Concurrency in Practice* by Brian Goetz.

We'll start with the following example, which creates 100,000 threads to increment a counter:

```
var counter = 0
val latch = CountDownLatch(100_000)
for (i in 1..100_000) {
    thread {
        counter++
        latch.countDown()
    }
}

latch.await()
println("Counter $counter")
```

If you have a bit of experience with concurrent programming, you'll understand right away why this code prints a number that is less than 100,000. The reason is the ++ operation is not atomic. So the more threads that try to increment our counter, the more chances for data races.

But, unlike Java, there's no `synchronized` keyword in Kotlin. The reason is that Kotlin designers believe that a language shouldn't be tailored to a particular concurrency model. Instead, there's a `synchronized()` function:

```
var counter = 0
val latch = CountDownLatch(100_000)
for (i in 1..100_000) {
    thread{
        synchronized(latch) {
            counter++
            latch.countDown()
        }
    }
}
```

```
latch.await()
println("Counter $counter")
```

Now our code prints `100000`, as expected.

If you really miss the synchronized methods from Java, there's the `@Synchronized` annotation in Kotlin. There's also no `volatile` keyword, but the `@Volatile` annotation instead.

Threads are expensive

There is a price to pay whenever we create a new thread. Each thread needs a new memory stack.

What if we simulate some work inside each thread by putting it to sleep?

In the following piece of code, we'll attempt to create 10,000 threads, each sleeping for a relatively short period of time:

```
val counter = AtomicInteger()
try {
    for (i in 0..10_000) {
        thread {
            counter.incrementAndGet()
            Thread.sleep(100)
        }
    }
} catch (oome: OutOfMemoryError) {
    println("Spawned ${counter.get()} threads before crashing")
    System.exit(-42)
}
```

Depending on your operation system, this will result in either `OutOfMemoryError` or the entire system becoming very slow. Of course, there are ways to limit how many threads are run at once, using the **executors API** from Java 5.

We create a new thread pool of a specified size:

```
// Try setting this to 1, number of cores, 100, 2000, 3000 and see what
happens
val pool = Executors.newFixedThreadPool(100)
```

Now we would like to submit a new task. We're doing this by calling `pool.submit()`:

```
val counter = AtomicInteger(0)

val start = System.currentTimeMillis()
for (i in 1..10_000) {
    pool.submit {
        // Do something
        counter.incrementAndGet()

        // Simulate wait on IO
        Thread.sleep(100)

        // Do something again
        counter.incrementAndGet()
    }
}
```

Then we need to make sure that the pool terminates, by using the following lines:

```
pool.awaitTermination(20, TimeUnit.SECONDS)
pool.shutdown()

println("Took me ${System.currentTimeMillis() - start} millis to complete
${counter.get() / 2} tasks")
```

Notice that it took us 20 seconds to complete. That's because a new task cannot begin until previous tasks *woke up* and completed their job.

And that's exactly what happens in multithreaded systems, which is not concurrent enough.

In the next section, we'll discuss how coroutines try to solve this problem.

Coroutines

In addition to the threading model provided by Java, Kotlin also introduces a coroutines model. Coroutines might be considered lightweight threads, and we'll see what advantages they provide over an existing model of threads shortly.

The first thing you need to know is that coroutines are not part of the language. They are simply another library provided by JetBrains. For that reason, if we want to use them, we need to specify so in our Gradle configuration file, `build.gradle`:

```
dependencies {
    ...
    compile "org.jetbrains.kotlinx:kotlinx-coroutines-core:0.21"
    ...
}
```

As of Kotlin 1.2, coroutines are still considered experimental. This doesn't mean that they don't work well, though, as some might think. It only means that some parts of the API may still change in the next versions.

What could change? For example, in 0.18, an Actor, which we'll discuss later in this chapter, exposed a channel member. In 0.21, this member was made private and a method was added instead. So instead of calling `actor.channel.send()`, you would call `actor.send()`.

 It's fine if you're not aware what *actor* or *channel* mean at this point. We'll cover those terms in the following sections shortly.

For that reason, after you add this dependency and start using them, you may get warnings during compilation or in your IDE:

```
The feature "coroutines" is experimental
```

You can hide those warnings with the following Gradle configuration:

```
kotlin {
    experimental {
        coroutines 'enable'
    }
}
```

Now, let's get started with coroutines.

Starting coroutines

We've already seen how to start a new thread in Kotlin. Now let's start a new coroutine instead.

We'll create almost the same example we did with threads. Each coroutine will increment some counter, sleep for a while to emulate some kind of IO, and then increment it again:

```kotlin
val latch = CountDownLatch(10_000)
val c = AtomicInteger()

val start = System.currentTimeMillis()
for (i in 1..10_000) {
    launch(CommonPool) {
        c.incrementAndGet()
        delay(100)
        c.incrementAndGet()
        latch.countDown()
    }
}

latch.await(10, TimeUnit.SECONDS)

println("Executed ${c.get() / 2} coroutines in ${System.currentTimeMillis()
- start}ms")
```

The first way of starting a new coroutine is by using the launch() function. Again, note that this is simply another function and not a language construct.

This function receives one argument: context: CoroutineContext.

Under the hood, coroutines still use a thread pool. For that reason, we can specify which thread pool to use. CommonPool is a singleton provided by the library out of the box.

Another interesting point here is called to the delay() function we use to simulate some IO bound work, like fetching something from a database or over the network.

Like the Thread.sleep() method, it puts the current coroutine to sleep. But unlike Thread.sleep(), other coroutines can work while this one sleeps soundly. This is due to the fact that delay() is marked with a suspend keyword, which we'll discuss in the section *Waiting for coroutines*.

If you run this code, you'll see that the task takes about 200 ms with coroutines, while with threads it either took 20 seconds or ran out of memory. And we didn't have to change our code that much. That's all thanks to the fact that coroutines are highly concurrent in their nature. They can be suspended without blocking the thread that runs them. Not blocking a thread is great, because we can use less OS threads (which are expensive) to do more work.

But of course, they're not magical. Let's create a **Factory** for our coroutines, which will be able to produce either a short-running or long-running coroutine:

```
object CoroutineFactory {
    fun greedyLongCoroutine(index: Int) = async {
        var uuid = UUID.randomUUID()
        for (i in 1..100_000) {
            val newUuid = UUID.randomUUID()

            if (newUuid < uuid) {
                uuid = newUuid
            }
        }

        println("Done greedyLongCoroutine $index")
        latch.countDown()
    }

    fun shortCoroutine(index: Int) = async {
        println("Done shortCoroutine $index!")
        latch.countDown()
    }
}
```

We don't actually need the **Factory Method** design pattern here, but it's a nice reminder. You'll understand why the long-running coroutine is called **greedy** very soon.

If you don't remember what the Factory Method is about, you should check `Chapter 2`, *Working with Creational Patterns*, section *Factory method* again. In short, it's a method that returns an object. Which object does it return in our case? It's a job representing a coroutine, of course! We'll explain what job is for shortly.

Jobs

The result of running an asynchronous task is called a job. Much like the `Thread` object represents an actual OS thread, the `job` object represents an actual coroutine. A job has a simple lifecycle.

It can be either as follows:

- New: Created, but not started yet.
- Active: Just created by `launch()` function, for example. This is the default state.
- Completed: Everything went well.
- Canceled: Something went wrong.

There are two more states relevant to jobs that have child jobs:

- Completing: Waiting to finish executing children before completing
- Canceling: Waiting to finish executing children before canceling

If you want to understand more about parent and child jobs, just jump to the *Parent jobs* section in this chapter.

Job also has some useful methods, which we'll discuss in the following sections.

Coroutine starvation

We'll call both the `greedyLongCoroutine()` and `shortCoroutine()` methods 10 times each and wait until they finish:

```
val latch = CountDownLatch(10 * 2)
fun main(args: Array<String>) {

    for (i in 1..10) {
        CoroutineFactory.greedyLongCoroutine(i)
    }

    for (i in 1..10) {
        CoroutineFactory.shortCoroutine(i)
    }

    latch.await(10, TimeUnit.SECONDS)
}
```

It's obvious that since coroutines are asynchronous, we'll see first 10 lines of the short coroutine then 10 lines of the long coroutine:

```
Done greedyLongCoroutine 2
Done greedyLongCoroutine 4
Done greedyLongCoroutine 3
Done greedyLongCoroutine 5
Done shortCoroutine 1! <= You should have finished long ago!
Done shortCoroutine 2!
Done shortCoroutine 3!
Done shortCoroutine 4!
Done shortCoroutine 5!
Done shortCoroutine 6!
Done shortCoroutine 7!
Done shortCoroutine 8!
Done shortCoroutine 9!
Done shortCoroutine 10!
Done greedyLongCoroutine 6
Done greedyLongCoroutine 7
Done greedyLongCoroutine 1
Done greedyLongCoroutine 8
Done greedyLongCoroutine 9
Done greedyLongCoroutine 10
```

Oops... That's not what you would expect. It seems like the long coroutines block the short coroutines somehow.

The reason for this behavior is that there is still an *event loop* based on the *thread pool* behind the coroutines. Since the CPU of my laptop has four cores, four long coroutines took all its resources, and until they finish their CPU-bound task, no other coroutine can start. To understand this better, let's dive deeper into how coroutines work.

Coroutines under the hood

So, we've mentioned a couple of times the following facts:

- Coroutines are like light-weight threads. They need less resources that regular threads, so you can create more of them.
- Coroutines use thread pool behind the scenes.
- Instead of blocking an entire thread, coroutine suspends.

But how does that actually work?

Let's see an abstract example. How would we compose a user profile?

```
fun profile(id: String): Profile {
    val bio = fetchBioOverHttp(id) // takes 1s
    val picture = fetchPictureFromDB(id) // takes 100ms
    val friends = fetchFriendsFromDB(id) // takes 500ms
    return Profile(bio, picture)
}
```

Summing up, our function now takes around 1.6 seconds to complete.

But we've learned about threads. Let's refactor this function to use them instead!

```
fun profile(id: String): Profile {
    val bio = fetchBioOverHttpThread(id) // still takes 1s
    val picture = fetchPictureFromDBThread(id) // still takes 100ms
    val friends = fetchFriendsFromDBThread(id) // still takes 500ms
    return Profile(bio, picture)
}
```

Now our function takes on average 1 second, the slowest of the three requests. But since we created a thread for each request, our memory footprint is three times larger. And we risk running out of memory quickly.

So, let's use a thread pool to limit the memory footprint:

```
fun profile(id: String): Profile {
    val bio = fetchBioOverHttpThreadPool()
    val picture = fetchPictureFromDBThreadPool()
    val friends = fetchFriendsFromDBThreadPool()
    return Profile(bio, picture)
}
```

But what happens if we call this function 100 times now? If we have a thread pool of 10 threads, the first 10 requests will get into the pool and the 11th will get stuck until the first one finishes. That means we can serve three users simultaneously, and the fourth one will wait until the first one gets his/her results.

How is that different with coroutines? Coroutines break your methods into even smaller methods.

Let's dive deeper into one of the functions to understand how it's done:

```
fun fetchBioOverHttp(id: String): Bio {
    doSomething() // 50ms
    val result = httpCall() // 900ms
    return Bio(result) // 50ms
}
```

That's one function that will take 1 second to execute.

What we can do, though, is mark `httpCall()` with the `suspend` keyword:

```
suspend fun httpCall(): Result {
    ...
}
```

When Kotlin compiler sees this keyword, it knows it can split and rewrite the function into two like this:

```
fun fetchBioOverHttp(id: String): Bio {
    doSomething() // 50ms
    httpCall() { // It was marked as suspend, so I can rewrite it!
        callback(it)
    } // Thread is released after 50ms
}

// This will be called after 950ms
fun callback(httpResult: Result) {
    return Bio(httpResult)
}
```

By doing that rewrite, we are able to release the thread that executes coroutines much sooner.

For a single user, that doesn't matter much. He will still get the results after 1 second.

But looking at the bigger picture, it means that by using the same amount of threads, we can serve 20 times more users, all thanks to the smart way Kotlin has rewritten our code.

Fixing starvation

Let's add another method to our Factory using the extension methods:

```
fun CoroutineFactory.longCoroutine(index: Int) = launch {
    var uuid = UUID.randomUUID()
    for (i in 1..100_000) {
```

```
        val newUuid = UUID.randomUUID()

        if (newUuid < uuid) {
            uuid = newUuid
        }

        if (i % 100 == 0) {
            yield()
        }
    }

    println("Done longCoroutine $index")
    latch.countDown()
}
```

We call this method instead in the first loop:

```
...
for (i in 1..10) {
    CoroutineFactory.longCoroutine(i)
}
...
```

And when we run it now, we get the output we expected in the first place:

```
Done shortCoroutine 0!
Done shortCoroutine 1!
Done shortCoroutine 2!
Done shortCoroutine 3!
Done shortCoroutine 5!
Done shortCoroutine 6!
Done shortCoroutine 7!
Done shortCoroutine 8!
Done shortCoroutine 9!
Done shortCoroutine 4!
Done longCoroutine 4 <= That makes more sense
Done longCoroutine 2
Done longCoroutine 3
Done longCoroutine 9
Done longCoroutine 5
Done longCoroutine 1
Done longCoroutine 10
Done longCoroutine 6
Done longCoroutine 7
Done longCoroutine 8
```

Now let's understand what actually happened. We used a new function: `yield()`. We could have called `yield()` on every loop iteration, but decided to do that every 100th one. It *asks* the pool whether there is anybody else that wants to do some work. If there's nobody else, the execution of the current coroutine will resume. Otherwise, another coroutine will start or resume from the point where it stopped earlier.

Note that without the `suspend` keyword on our function or a coroutine generator, such as `launch()`, we can't call `yield()`. That's true for any function marked with `suspend`: it should be called either from another `suspend` function or from a coroutine.

Waiting for a coroutine

Up until now, to let our asynchronous code complete, we've used either `Thread.sleep()` or `CountDownLatch`. But there are better options with threads and coroutines. Much like Thread, a job has the `join()` function. By invoking it, we can wait for the execution of the coroutine to complete.

Take a look at the following code:

```
val j = launch(CommonPool) {
    for (i in 1..10_000) {
        if (i % 1000 == 0) {
            println(i)
            yield()
        }
    }
}
```

Although it should have printed 10 lines, it doesn't print anything, actually. That's because our main thread terminates before giving a coroutine a chance to start.

By adding the following lines, our example will print the expected results:

```
runBlocking {
    j.join()
}
```

What about this `runBlocking`, you ask? Remember that we could call `yield()` only from another coroutine because it's a *suspending function*? The same is true for `join()`. Since our main method is not a coroutine, we need to have a **bridge** between our regular code, that is not a suspending function and coroutines. This function does exactly that.

Canceling a coroutine

If you are a Java developer, you may know that stopping a thread is quite complicated.

For example, the `Thread.stop()` method is deprecated. There's `Thread.interrupt()`, but not all threads are checking this flag, not to mention setting your own `volatile` flag, which is often suggested but is very cumbersome.

If you're using a thread pool, you'll get `Future`, which has the `cancel(boolean mayInterruptIfRunning)` method. In Kotlin, the `launch()` function returns a job.

This job can be canceled. The same rules as the previous example apply, though. If your coroutine never calls another `suspend` method or yields, it will disregard `cancel()`.

To demonstrate that, we'll create one *nice* coroutine that yields once in a while:

```
val cancellable = launch {
    try {
        for (i in 1..1000) {
            println("Cancellable: $i")
            computeNthFibonacci(i)
            yield()
        }
    }
    catch (e: CancellationException) {
        e.printStackTrace()
    }
}
```

And another one that doesn't yield:

```
val notCancellable = launch {
    for (i in 1..1000) {
        println("Not cancellable $i")
        computeNthFibonacci(i)
    }
}
```

We'll try to cancel both:

```
println("Canceling cancellable")
cancellable.cancel()
println("Canceling not cancellable")
notCancellable.cancel()
```

And wait for the results:

```
runBlocking {
    cancellable.join()
    notCancellable.join()
}
```

A few interesting points:

1. Canceling the *nice* coroutine doesn't happen immediately. It may still print a line or two before getting canceled.
2. We can catch `CancellationException`, but our coroutine will be marked as canceled anyway.

Returning results

Calling `launch()` is much like calling a function that returns `Unit`. But most of our functions return some kind of result. For that purpose, we have the `async()` function. It also launches a coroutine, but instead of returning a job, it returns `Deferred<T>`, where `T` is the type you expect to get later.

Think of a situation where you would like to fetch the user's profile from one source and their history from another. It may be two DB queries, or a network call to two remote services, or any combination.

You must show both the profile and the history, but you don't know which returns first. Usually, retrieving the profile is faster. But sometimes there may be a delay, since profiles are updated often and the history will return first.

We run one coroutine that will return the user's profile string in our case:

```
val userProfile = async {
    delay(Random().nextInt(100))
    "Profile"
}
```

We'll run another to return the history. For simplicity, we'll just return a list of Ints:

```
val userHistory = async {
    delay(Random().nextInt(200))
    listOf(1, 2, 3)
}
```

To wait for the results, we use the `await()` function:

```
runBlocking {
    println("User profile is ${userProfile.await()} and his history is
${userHistory.await()}")
}
```

Setting timeouts

What if, as happens in some cases, fetching the user's profile takes too long? What if we decided that if the profile takes more than 0.5 seconds to return, we'll just show *no profile*?

This can be achieved using the `withTimeout()` function:

```
val coroutine = async {
    withTimeout(500, TimeUnit.MILLISECONDS) {
        try {
            val time = Random().nextInt(1000)

            println("It will take me $time to do")

            delay(time)

            println("Returning profile")
            "Profile"
        }
        catch (e: TimeoutCancellationException) {
            e.printStackTrace()
        }
    }
}
```

We set the timeout to be 500 milliseconds, and our coroutine will delay for between 0 and 1,000 milliseconds, giving it a 50 percent chance to fail.

We'll await results from the coroutine and see what happens:

```
val result = try {
    coroutine.await()
}
catch (e: TimeoutCancellationException) {
    "No Profile"
}

println(result)
```

Here we benefit from the fact that `try` is an expression in Kotlin. So we can return a result immediately from it.

If the coroutine manages to return before the timeout, the value of `result` becomes *profile*. Otherwise, we receive `TimeoutCancellationException`, and set the value of `result` to *no profile*.

The interesting part is that our coroutine always receives `TimeoutCancellationException`, which we can handle. And in case of a timeout, *returning profile* will never be printed.

A combination of timeouts and try-catch expressions is a really powerful tool that allows us to create robust interactions.

Parent jobs

What if we want to cancel more than one coroutine at the same time? That's where parent jobs come into play. Remember that `launch()` receives `CoroutineContext`, that's usually `CommonPool`? It can also receive other parameters, which will see shortly.

We'll start with a suspending function that works for some time:

```
suspend fun produceBeautifulUuid(): String {
    try {
        val uuids = List(1000) {
            yield()
            UUID.randomUUID()
        }

        println("Coroutine done")
        return uuids.sorted().first().toString()
    } catch (t: CancellationException) {
        println("Got cancelled")
    }

    return ""
}
```

We would like to launch 10 of these and cancel them after only 100 ms.

For that, we'll use a parent job:

```
val parentJob = Job()

List(10) {
    async(CommonPool + parentJob) {
        produceBeautifulUuid()
    }
}

delay(100)
parentJob.cancel()
delay(1000) // Wait some more time
```

As you can see, a parent job is simply a job. We pass it to the `async()` function. We can use the + sign due to the fact that `CoroutineContext` has overloaded the `plus()` function. You can also specify it using named arguments:

```
async(CommonPool, parent= parentJob)
```

Once we invoke `cancel()` on parent job, all of its children are canceled too.

Channels

Up until now, we learned how to spawn coroutines and control them. But what if two coroutines need to communicate with each other?

In Java, threads communicate either by using the `wait()`/`notify()`/`notifyAll()` pattern or by using one of the rich set of classes from the java.util.concurrent package. For example: `BlockingQueue` or `Exchanger`.

In Kotlin, as you may have noticed, there are no `wait()`/`notify()` methods. But there are channels, which are very similar to `BlockingQueue`. But instead of blocking a thread, channels suspend a coroutine, which is a lot cheaper.

To understand channels better, let's create a simple game of two players that will throw random numbers at each other. If your number is greater, you win. Otherwise, you lose the round:

```
fun player(name: String,
           input: Channel<Int>,
           output: Channel<Int>) = launch {
```

```
for (m in input) {
    val d = Random().nextInt(100)
    println("$name got $m, ${if (d > m) "won" else "lost" }")

    delay(d)
    output.send(d)
}
}
```

Each player has two channels. One is used to receive data, the other to send it.

We can iterate over a channel with a regular for-loop, which will suspend until the next value is received.

When we want to send our results to the other player, we simply use the `send()` method.

Now let's play this game for one second:

```
fun main(vararg args: String) {
    val p1p2 = Channel<Int>()
    val p2p1 = Channel<Int>()

    val player1 = player("Player 1", p2p1, p1p2)
    val player2 = player("Player 2", p1p2, p2p1)

    runBlocking {
        p2p1.send(0)
        delay(1000)
    }
}
```

Our output may look something like this:

```
. . .
Player 1 got 62, won
Player 2 got 65, lost
Player 1 got 29, lost
Player 2 got 9, won
Player 1 got 46, won
Player 2 got 82, lost
Player 1 got 81, lost
. . .
```

As you can see, channels are a convenient and type-safe way to communicate between different coroutines. But we had to define the channels manually, and pass them in the correct order. In the next two sections, we'll see how this can be further simplified.

Producers

In Chapter 7, *Staying Reactive*, which was dedicated to reactive programming, we discussed Observable and subject that were producing streams of values. Much in the same way, Kotlin provides us with the produce() function.

This function creates coroutine is backed up by ReceiveChannel<T>, where T is the type the coroutine produces:

```
val publisher: ReceiveChannel<Int> = produce {
        for (i in 2018 downTo 1970) { // Years back to Unix
            send(i)
            delay(20)
        }
}
```

In Rx there's the onNext() method that we covered in Chapter 7, *Staying Reactive*.

Producers have a send() function, which is very similar.

Much like the Rx Observable that provided the subscribe() method, this channel, has the consumeEach() function:

```
publisher.consumeEach {
    println("Got $it")
}
```

It prints the following:

```
Got 35
Got 34
Got 33
Got 32
Got 31
Got 30
Got 29
```

Another great ability that channels provide is select().

If we have more than one producer, we can subscribe to their channels, and take the first result available:

```
val firstProducer = produce<String> {
    delay(Random().nextInt(100))
    send("First")
}
```

```
val secondProducer = produce<String> {
    delay(Random().nextInt(100))
    send("Second")
}

val winner = select<String> {
    firstProducer.onReceive {
        it.toLowerCase()
    }
    secondProducer.onReceive {
        it.toUpperCase()
    }
}

println(winner)
```

This will randomly print First or Second.

Note that select() happens only once. A common mistake is to have select on two coroutines that produce a stream of data, without wrapping it in a loop:

```
// Producer 1
val firstProducer = produce {
    for (c in 'a'..'z') {
        delay(Random().nextInt(100))
        send(c.toString())
    }
}

// Producer 2
val secondProducer = produce {
    for (c in 'A'..'Z') {
        delay(Random().nextInt(100))
        send(c.toString())
    }
}

// Receiver
println(select<String> {
    firstProducer.onReceive {
        it
    }
    secondProducer.onReceive {
        it
    }
})
```

Instead of printing the alphabet, this will only print either "a" or "A," and then exit. Make sure your `select()` is wrapped in a loop.

This will print the first 10 characters it receives:

```
// Receiver
for (i in 1..10) {
    println(select<String> {
        firstProducer.onReceive {
            it
        }
        secondProducer.onReceive {
            it
        }
    })
}
```

Another option is to signal using the `close()` function:

```
// Producer 2
val secondProducer = produce {
    for (c in 'A'..'Z') {
        delay(Random().nextInt(100))
        send(c.toString())
    }
    close()
}
```

And use `onReceiveOrNull()` inside the receiver:

```
// Receiver
while(true) {
    val result = select<String?> {
        firstProducer.onReceiveOrNull {
            it
        }
        secondProducer.onReceiveOrNull {
            it
        }
    }

    if (result == null) {
        break
    }
    else {
```

```
        println(result)
    }
}
```

This option will print characters until the first of the producers decide to close the channel.

Actors

The last *building block* introduced in this chapter is actors. Similar to `producer()`, `actor()` is a coroutine bound to a channel. But instead of a channel going *out* of the coroutine, there's a channel going *into* the coroutine. If you think that was too academic, read on for another explanation.

So what is an actor, anyway? Let's look at an interaction between Michael and me, an imaginary product manager, who happens to be a canary, as you may remember from `Chapter 4`, *Getting Familiar with Behavioral Patterns*. Michael has a list of tasks that need to be completed before the end of the sprint/week/month. And he simply throws them at me, in the hope that I'll do my magic and translate some vague specifications into a working code. He's not waiting for my response. He just expects that eventually, it will happen—and sooner rather than later. For Michael, I'm an actor. Not because I attended an acting school, but because I act upon his request.

If you've worked with Scala, or some other programming language that has actors, you may be familiar with a slightly different actor model from what we've described. In some implementations, actors have both inbound and outbound channels (often called mailboxes). But it Kotlin, an actor has only an inbound mailbox.

To create a new actor, we use the `actor()` function:

```
data class Task (val description: String)
val me = actor<Task> {
    while (!isClosedForReceive) {
        println(receive().description.repeat(10))
    }
}
```

Note that the same way that `select()` works, unless we wrap an actor's `receive()` into some kind of loop, it will execute only once. If you'll attempt to send it to a closed channel, you get `ClosedSendChannelException`.

You communicate with actors using `send()`:

```
// Imagine this is Michael the PM
fun michael(actor: SendChannel<Task>) {
    runBlocking {
        // He has some range of tasks
        for (i in 'a'..'z') {
            // That he's sending to me
            actor.send(Task(i.toString()))
        }
        // And when he's done with the list, he let's me know
        actor.close()
        // That doesn't mean I'm done working on it, though
    }
}

// And he's calling me
michael(me)
```

Another pattern for an actor is to use the `receiveOrNull()` function:

```
val meAgain = actor<Task> {
    var next = receiveOrNull()

    while (next != null) {
        println(next.description.toUpperCase())
        next = receiveOrNull()
    }
}

// Michael still can call me in the same manner
michael(meAgain)
```

As you can see, instead of checking whether the actor's channel has been closed, our cue is receiving null on the channel. This approach may be preferable, if the actor receives tasks from many *managers*.

The third option, which is the most preferable one usually, is to iterate over the channel:

```
val meWithRange = actor<Task> {
    for (t in channel) {
        println(t.description)
    }

    println("Done everything")
```

```
    }

    michael(meWithRange)
```

As you can see, this is the cleanest implementation of the three.

Actors are a very useful for background tasks that need to maintain some kind of state. For example, you could create an actor that would generate reports. It will receive what kind of report to generate, and will make sure that only one report is generated at the same time:

```
data class ReportRequest(val name: String,
                                val from: LocalDate,
                                val to: LocalDate)
val reportsActor = actor<ReportRequest>(capacity=100) {
    for (req in this) {
        generateReport(req)
    }
}
```

It is often a good idea to limit the capacity of messages the actor can receive.

Then we can send this actor what type of report to produce:

```
reportsActor.send(ReportRequest("Monthly Report",
        LocalDate.of(2018, 1, 1),
        LocalDate.of(2018, 1, 31)))
```

Summary

In this chapter, we covered how to create threads and coroutines in Kotlin, and the benefits of coroutines.

Kotlin has simplified syntax for creating threads, compared to Java. But they still have the overhead of memory and often performance. Coroutines are able to solve these issues; use coroutines whenever you need to execute some code concurrently.

If you want to communicate between two coroutines, use channels.

Kotlin also offers actors with the `actor()` function, which also spins a coroutine that has an inbound stream attached to it to process events. And if you need to create a stream of values, you can use the `produce()` function.

In the next chapter, we'll discuss how we can use these concurrency primitives to create scalable and robust systems that suit our needs.

Designed for Concurrency

9

In this chapter, we'll discuss the most common concurrency design patterns, implemented with coroutines, and how coroutines can synchronize their execution.

Concurrent design patterns help us to manage many tasks at once. Yeah, I know, that's what we did in the last chapter. That's because some of those design patterns are already built into the language.

In this chapter, we'll briefly cover design patterns and other concurrent design patterns that you'll need to implement by yourself, with little effort.

We will be covering the following topics in this chapter:

- Active Object
- Deferred value
- Barrier
- Scheduler
- Pipelines
- Fan out
- Fan in
- Buffered channels
- Unbiased select
- Mutex
- Select on close
- Sidekick channel
- Deferred channel

Active Object

This design pattern allows a method to be executed in a safe way on another thread. Guess what else is being executed on another thread?

You're totally right: `actor()`.

So, it's one of those design patterns that is already built into the language. Or, to be precise, into one of the accommodating libraries.

We've already seen how to send data to `actor()`. But how do we receive data from it?

One way is to supply it with a channel for output:

```
fun activeActor(out: SendChannel<String>) = actor<Int> {
    for (i in this) {
        out.send(i.toString().reversed())
    }
    out.close()
}
```

Remember to close the output channel when you're done.

Testing

To test the **Active Object** pattern, we'll launch two jobs. One will send data to our actor:

```
val channel = Channel<String>()
val actor = activeActor(channel)

val j1 = launch {
    for (i in 42..53) {
        actor.send(i)
    }
    actor.close()
}
```

And another will wait for output on the outbound channel:

```
val j2 = launch {
    for (i in channel) {
        println(i)
    }
}
```

```
j1.join()
j2.join()
```

Deferred value

We've already met deferred values in Chapter 8, *Threads and Coroutines*, in the *Returning results* section. Deferred is the result of the async() function, for example. You may also know them as *Futures* from Java or Scala, or as *Promises* from JavaScript.

Interestingly enough, Deferred is a **Proxy** design pattern that we've met in previous chapters.

Much as the Kotlin Sequence is very similar to the Java8 Stream, Kotlin Deferred is very similar to Java Future. You'll rarely need to create your own Deferred. Usually, you would work with the one returned from async().

In cases where you do need to return a placeholder for a value that would be evaluated in the future, you can do it:

```
val deferred = CompletableDeferred<String>()

launch {
    delay(100)
    if (Random().nextBoolean()) {
        deferred.complete("OK")
    }
    else {
        deferred.completeExceptionally(RuntimeException())
    }
}

println(deferred.await())
```

This code will print OK half of the time, and throw RuntimeException the other half of the time.

Make sure that you always complete your deferred. It is usually a good idea to wrap any code containing deferred into a try...catch block.

It is also possible to cancel a deferred if you're no longer interested in its results. Simply call cancel() on it:

```
deferred.cancel()
```

Barrier

The Barrier design pattern provides us with the means to wait for multiple concurrent tasks before proceeding further. A common use case is composing objects from different sources.

Take, for example, the following class:

```
data class FavoriteCharacter(val name: String, val catchphrase: String, val
repeats: Int)
```

Assume that we're fetching name, catchphrase, and number. This catchphrase is being repeated from three different sources.

The most basic way would be to use CountDownLatch, as we did in some of the previous examples:

```
val latch = CountDownLatch(3)

var name: String? = null
launch {
    delay(Random().nextInt(100))
    println("Got name")
    name = "Inigo Montoya"
    latch.countDown()
}

var catchphrase = ""
launch {
    delay(Random().nextInt(100))
    println("Got catchphrase")
    catchphrase = "Hello. My name is Inigo Montoya. You killed my father.
Prepare to die."
    latch.countDown()
}

var repeats = 0
launch {
    delay(Random().nextInt(100))
    println("Got repeats")
    repeats = 6
    latch.countDown()
}

latch.await()

println("${name} says: ${catchphrase.repeat(repeats)}")
```

You'll notice that the order of the async tasks completing is changing:

```
Got name
Got catchphrase
Got repeats
```

But in the end, we always print the same result:

Inigo Montoya says: Hello. My name is Inigo Montoya. ...

But this solution brings a lot of problems. We need to work with mutable variables and either set defaults for them or use nulls.

Also, this would work as long as we use closures. What if our functions were longer than a few lines?

CountDownLatch

We could pass them the latch, of course. The latch, which we've already seen a couple of times, allows one thread to wait until the other threads have completed working:

```
private fun getName(latch: CountDownLatch) = launch {
    ...
    latch.countDown()
}
```

But it's not a clear separation of concerns. Do we really want to specify how this function should be synchronized?

Let's have a second take:

```
private fun getName() = async {
    delay(Random().nextInt(100))
    println("Got name")
    "Inigo Montoya"
}

private fun getCatchphrase() = async {
    delay(Random().nextInt(100))
    println("Got catchphrase")
    "Hello. My name is Inigo Montoya. You killed my father. Prepare to
die."
}

private fun getRepeats() = async {
    delay(Random().nextInt(100))
```

```
    println("Got repeats")
    6
}
```

Just a reminder, `fun getRepeats() = async { ... }` has nothing magical in it. Its longer equivalent is:

```
private fun getCatchphrase(): Deferred<String> {
    return async {
        ...
    }
}
```

We can call our code to get the same results as before:

```
val name = getName()
val catchphrase = getCatchphrase()
val repeats = getRepeats()

println("${name.await()} says:
${catchphrase.await().repeat(repeats.await())}")
```

But we can improve it further by using our old friend, data class.

Data class as Barrier

Now our data class is the Barrier:

```
val character = FavoriteCharacter(getName().await(),
getCatchphrase().await(), getRepeats().await())

// Will happen only when everything is ready
with(character) {
    println("$name says: ${catchphrase.repeat(repeats)}")
}
```

The additional benefit of data classes as Barriers is the ability to destructure them easily:

```
val (name, catchphrase, repeats) = character
println("$name says: ${catchphrase.repeat(repeats)}")
```

This works well if the type of data we receive from different asynchronous tasks is widely different. In this example, we receive both `String` and `Int`.

In some cases, we receive the same types of data from different sources.

For example, let's ask Michael (our canary product owner), Jake (our barista), and me who our favorite movie character is:

```
object Michael {
    fun getFavoriteCharacter() = async {
        // Doesn't like to think much
        delay(Random().nextInt(10))
        FavoriteCharacter("Terminator", "Hasta la vista, baby", 1)
    }
}

object Jake {
    fun getFavoriteCharacter() = async {
        // Rather thoughtful barista
        delay(Random().nextInt(100) + 10)
        FavoriteCharacter("Don Vito Corleone", "I'm going to make him an
offer he can't refuse", 1)
    }
}

object Me {
    fun getFavoriteCharacter() = async {
        // I already prepared the answer!
        FavoriteCharacter("Inigo Montoya", "Hello, my name is...", 6)
    }
}
```

In that case, we can use a list to gather the results:

```
val favoriteCharacters = listOf(Me.getFavoriteCharacter().await(),
        Michael.getFavoriteCharacter().await(),
        Jake.getFavoriteCharacter().await())

println(favoriteCharacters)
```

Scheduler

This is another concept we discussed briefly in `Chapter 8`, *Threads and Coroutines*, in the *Starting a coroutine* section.

Remember how our `launch()` or `async()` could receive `CommonPool`?

Here's an example to remind you that you could specify it explicitly:

```
// Same as launch {}
launch(CommonPool) {
    ...
}

// Same as async {}
val result = async(CommonPool) {
    ...
}
```

This `CommonPool` is a Scheduler design pattern in a bad disguise. Many async tasks may be mapped to the same Scheduler.

Run the following code:

```
val r1 = async(CommonPool) {
    for (i in 1..1000) {
        println(Thread.currentThread().name)
        yield()
    }
}

r1.await()
```

What is interesting is the fact that the same coroutine is picked up by different threads:

```
ForkJoinPool.commonPool-worker-2
ForkJoinPool.commonPool-worker-3
...
ForkJoinPool.commonPool-worker-3
ForkJoinPool.commonPool-worker-1
```

You can also specify the context as `Unconfined`:

```
val r1 = async(Unconfined) {
    ...
}
```

This will run the coroutine on the main thread. It prints:

```
main
main
...
```

You can also inherit context from your parent coroutine:

```
val r1 = async {
    for (i in 1..1000) {
        val parentThread = Thread.currentThread().name
        launch(coroutineContext) {
            println(Thread.currentThread().name == parentThread)
        }
        yield()
    }
}
```

Note though, that running in the same context doesn't mean that we run on the same thread.

You may ask yourself: what's the difference between inheriting the context and using Unconfined? We'll discuss this in detail in the next section.

Understanding contexts

To understand different contexts, let's look at the following code:

```
val r1 = async(Unconfined) {
    for (i in 1..1000) {
        println(Thread.currentThread().name)
        delay(1)
    }
}

r1.await()
```

Instead of yield(), we're using the delay() function, which also suspends the current coroutine.

But the output compared to yield() is different:

```
main
kotlinx.coroutines.DefaultExecutor
...
```

After calling delay() for the first time, the coroutine has switched context, and as a result, threads.

For that reason, using Unconfined is not recommended for CPU-intensive tasks or tasks that need to run on a particular thread, such as UI rendering.

You can also create your own thread pool for coroutines to run on:

```
val pool = newFixedThreadPoolContext(2, "My Own Pool")
val r1 = async(pool) {
    for (i in 1..1000) {
        println(Thread.currentThread().name)
        yield()
    }
}

r1.await()
pool.close()
```

It prints:

```
...
My Own Pool-2
My Own Pool-1
My Own Pool-2
My Own Pool-2
...
```

If you create your own thread pool, make sure that you either release it with `close()` or reuse it, since creating a new thread pool and holding to it is expensive in terms of resources.

Pipelines

In our `StoryLand`, the same lazy architect, me, is struggling with a problem. Back in `Chapter 4`, *Getting Familiar with Behavioral Patterns*, we wrote an HTML page parser. But it depends on whether somebody already fetched the pages to parse for us. It is also not very flexible.

What we would like is for one coroutine to produce an infinite stream of news, and for others to parse that stream in steps.

To start working with DOM, we'll need a library, such as `kotlinx.dom`. If you're using **Gradle**, make sure you add the following lines to your `build.gradle`:

```
repositories {
    ...
    jcenter()
}
```

```
dependencies {
    ...
    compile "org.jetbrains.kotlinx:kotlinx.dom:0.0.10"
}
```

Now, to the task at hand.

First, we would like to fetch news pages once in a while. For that, we'll have a producer:

```
fun producePages() = produce {
    fun getPages(): List<String> {
        // This should actually fetch something
        return listOf("<html><body><H1>Cool stuff</H1></body></html>",
                "<html><body><H1>Event more
stuff</H1></body></html>").shuffled()
    }
    while (this.isActive) {
        val pages = getPages()
        for (p in pages) {
            send(p)
        }
        delay(TimeUnit.SECONDS.toMillis(5))
    }
}
```

We use `shuffled()` here so the order of the list elements won't be the same all the time.

The `isActive` flag will be true as long as the coroutine is running and hasn't been canceled. It is good practice to check this property in loops that may run for a long time, so they could be stopped between iterations.

Each time we receive new titles, we send them downstream.

Since tech news isn't updated very often. We can check for updates only once in a while, using `delay()`. In the actual code, the delay would probably be minutes, if not hours.

The next step is creating **Document Object Model (DOM)** out of those raw strings containing HTML. For that we'll have a second producer, this one receiving a channel that connects it to the first one:

```
fun produceDom(pages: ReceiveChannel<String>) = produce {

    fun parseDom(page: String): Document {
        return kotlinx.dom.parseXml(page.toSource())
    }

    for (p in pages) {
```

```
            send(parseDom(p))
        }
    }
```

We can use the `for` loop to iterate over the channel as long as more data is coming. This is a very elegant way of consuming data from a channel.

In this producer, we finally make use of the DOM parser we imported a while ago. We also introduced an extension function on `String` for our convenience:

```
private fun String.toSource(): InputSource {
    return InputSource(StringReader(this))
}
```

That's because `parseXml()` expects `InputSource` as its input. Basically, this is an **Adapter** design pattern in action:

```
fun produceTitles(parsedPages: ReceiveChannel<Document>) = produce {
    fun getTitles(dom: Document): List<String> {
        val h1 = dom.getElementsByTagName("H1")
        return h1.asElementList().map {
            it.textContent
        }
    }

    for (page in parsedPages) {
        for (t in getTitles(page)) {
            send(t)
        }
    }
}
```

We're looking for the headers, hence `getElementsByTagName("H1")`. For each header found, and there may be more than one, we get its text with `textContent`.

Finally, we're sending each header from each page to the next in line.

Establishing a pipeline

Now, to establish our pipeline:

```
val pagesProducer = producePages()

val domProducer = produceDom(pagesProducer)
```

```
val titleProducer = produceTitles(domProducer)

runBlocking {
    titleProducer.consumeEach {
        println(it)
    }
}
```

We have the following:

```
pagesProducer |> domProducer |> titleProducer |> output
```

A pipeline is a great way to break a long process into smaller steps. Note that each producing coroutine is a pure function, so it's also easy to test and reason about.

The entire pipeline could be stopped by calling `cancel()` on the first coroutine in line.

We can achieve an even nicer API by using the extension functions:

```
private fun ReceiveChannel<Document>.titles(): ReceiveChannel<String> {
    val channel = this
    fun getTitles(dom: Document): List<String> {
        val h1 = dom.getElementsByTagName("H1")
        return h1.asElementList().map {
            it.textContent
        }
    }

    return produce {
        for (page in channel) {
            for (t in getTitles(page)) {
                send(t)
            }
        }
    }
}

private fun ReceiveChannel<String>.dom(): ReceiveChannel<Document> {
    val channel = this
    return produce() {
        for (p in channel) {
            send(kotlinx.dom.parseXml(p.toSource()))
        }
    }
}
```

Then we can call our code like this:

```
runBlocking {
    producePages().dom().titles().consumeEach {
        println(it)
    }
}
```

Kotlin really excels at creating expressive and fluent APIs.

The fan-out design pattern

What if the amount of work at different steps in our pipeline is very different?

For example, it takes a lot more time to fetch the HTML than to parse it. Or what if we don't have a pipeline at all, just a lot of tasks we would like to distribute between coroutines.

That's where the fan-out design pattern kicks in. The number of coroutines may read from the same channel, distributing the work.

We can have one coroutine produce some results:

```
private fun producePages() = produce {
    for (i in 1..10_000) {
        for (c in 'a'..'z') {
            send(i to "page$c")
        }
    }
}
```

And have a function that would create a coroutine that reads those results:

```
private fun consumePages(channel: ReceiveChannel<Pair<Int, String>>) =
async {
    for (p in channel) {
        println(p)
    }
}
```

This allows us to generate an arbitrary number of consumers:

```
val producer = producePages()

val consumers = List(10) {
```

```
        consumePages(producer)
    }

runBlocking {
    consumers.forEach {
        it.await()
    }
}
```

The fan-out design pattern allows us to efficiently distribute the work across a number of coroutines, threads, and CPUs.

The fan-in design pattern

It would be great if our coroutines could always make decisions by themselves. But what if they need to return some results from the computation to another coroutine?

The opposite of **fan-out** is the **fan-in** design pattern. Instead of multiple coroutines reading from the same channel, multiple coroutines can write their results to the same channel.

Imagine that you're reading news from two prominent tech resources: techBunch and theFerge.

Each resource produces the values at its own pace, and sends them over a channel:

```
private fun techBunch(collector: Channel<String>) = launch {
    repeat(10) {
        delay(Random().nextInt(1000))
        collector.send("Tech Bunch")
    }
}

private fun theFerge(collector: Channel<String>) = launch {
    repeat(10) {
        delay(Random().nextInt(1000))
        collector.send("The Ferge")
    }
}
```

By providing them with the same channel, we can combine their results:

```
val collector = Channel<String>()

techBunch(collector)
theFerge(collector)
```

```
runBlocking {
    collector.consumeEachIndexed {
        println("${it.index} Got news from ${it.value}")
    }
}
```

Combining the fan-out and fan-in design patterns is a good base for **Map/Reduce** algorithms.

To demonstrate that, we'll generate 10,000,000 random numbers and compute the maximum number among them by dividing this task multiple times.

First, to generate the list of 10,000,000 random integers:

```
val numbers = List(10_000_000) {
    Random().nextInt()
}
```

Managing workers

Now we'll have two types of workers:

- The divide worker will receive the list of numbers, determine the biggest number in the list, and send it over to the output channel:

```
fun divide(input: ReceiveChannel<List<Int>>,
           output: SendChannel<Int>) = async {
    var max = 0
    for (list in input) {
        for (i in list) {
            if (i > max) {
                max = i
                output.send(max)
            }
        }
    }
}
```

- The collector will listen to this channel and each time a new sub-max number arrives, will decide whether it's the all-time biggest:

```
fun collector() = actor<Int> {
    var max = 0
    for (i in this) {
        max = Math.max(max, i)
```

```
        }
        println(max)
    }
```

Now we only need to establish those channels:

```
val input = Channel<List<Int>>()
val output = collector()
val dividers = List(10) {
    divide(input, output)
}

launch {
    for (c in numbers.chunked(1000)) {
        input.send(c)
    }
    input.close()
}

dividers.forEach {
    it.await()
}

output.close()
```

Note that in this case, we don't gain performance benefits, and naive `numbers.max()` would produce better results. But the more data you need to collect, the more useful this pattern becomes.

Buffered channels

Up until now, all the channels that we used had a capacity of exactly one element.

This means that if you write to this channel but no one reads from it, the sender will be suspended:

```
val channel = Channel<Int>()

val j = launch {
    for (i in 1..10) {
        channel.send(i)
        println("Sent $i")
```

```
        }
    }

    j.join()
```

This code doesn't print anything because the coroutine is waiting for someone to read from the channel.

To avoid that, we can create a buffered channel:

```
val channel = Channel<Int>(5)
```

Now suspension will occur only when the channel capacity is reached.

It prints:

```
Sent 1
Sent 2
Sent 3
Sent 4
Sent 5
```

Since `produce()` and `actor()` are also backed up by a channel, we can make it buffered too:

```
val actor = actor<Int>(capacity = 5) {
    ...
}

val producer = produce<Int>(capacity = 10) {
    ...
}
```

Unbiased select

One of the most useful ways to work with channels is the `select {}` clause we saw in `Chapter 8`, *Threads and Coroutines*, in the *Producers* section.

But select is inherently biased. If two events happen at the same time, it will select the first clause.

In the following example, we'll have a producer that sends five values with a very short delay:

```
fun producer(name: String, repeats: Int) = produce {
    repeat(repeats) {
        delay(1)
        send(name)
    }
}
```

We'll create three such producers and see the results:

```
val repeats = 10_000
val p1 = producer("A", repeats)
val p2 = producer("B", repeats)
val p3 = producer("C", repeats)

val results = ConcurrentHashMap<String, Int>()
repeat(repeats) {
    val result = select<String> {
        p1.onReceive { it }
        p2.onReceive { it }
        p3.onReceive { it }
    }

    results.compute(result) { k, v ->
        if (v == null) {
            1
        }
        else {
            v + 1
        }
    }
}

println(results)
```

We run this code five times. Here are some of the results:

```
{A=8235, B=1620, C=145}
{A=7850, B=2062, C=88}
{A=7878, B=2002, C=120}
{A=8260, B=1648, C=92}
{A=7927, B=2011, C=62}
```

As you can see, A almost always wins, while C is always third. The more repeats you set, the larger the bias gets.

Now let's use `selectUnbiased` instead:

```
...
val result = selectUnbiased<String> {
    p1.onReceive { it }
    p2.onReceive { it }
    p3.onReceive { it }
}
...
```

The results of the first five executions may look like this:

```
{A=3336, B=3327, C=3337}
{A=3330, B=3332, C=3338}
{A=3334, B=3333, C=3333}
{A=3334, B=3336, C=3330}
{A=3332, B=3335, C=3333}
```

Not only are the numbers distributed more evenly now, but all clauses have an equal chance of being selected.

Mutexes

Also known as mutual exclusions, mutexes provide a means to protect a shared state.

Let's start with same, old, dreaded counter example:

```
var counter = 0

val jobs = List(10) {
    launch {
        repeat(1000) {
            counter++
            yield()
        }
    }
}

runBlocking {
    jobs.forEach {
        it.join()
    }
    println(counter)
}
```

As you've probably guessed, this prints anything but the result of `10*100`. Totally embarrassing.

To solve that, we introduce a mutex:

```
var counter = 0
val mutex = Mutex()

val jobs = List(10) {
    launch {
        repeat(1000) {
            mutex.lock()
            counter++
            mutex.unlock()
            yield()
        }
    }
}
```

Now our example always prints the correct number.

This is good for simple cases. But what if the code within the critical section (that is, between `lock()` and `unlock()`) throws an exception?

Then we'll have to wrap everything in `try...catch`, which is not very convenient:

```
repeat(1000) {
    try {
        mutex.lock()
        counter++
    } finally {
        mutex.unlock()
    }
    yield()
}
```

Exactly for that purpose, Kotlin also introduces `withLock()`:

```
...
repeat(1000) {
    mutex.withLock {
        counter++
    }
    yield()
}
...
```

Selecting on close

Reading from a channel using `select()` is nice until it gets closed.

You can see an example of that problem here:

```
val p1 = produce {
    repeat(10) {
        send("A")
    }
}

val p2 = produce {
    repeat(5) {
        send("B")
    }
}


runBlocking {
    repeat(15) {
        val result = selectUnbiased<String> {
            p1.onReceive {
                it
            }
            p2.onReceive {
                it
            }
        }

        println(result)
    }
}
```

Although the numbers add up, we may often receive `ClosedReceiveChannelException` running this code. That's because the second producer has fewer items, and as soon as it finishes, it will close its channel.

To avoid that, we can use `onReceiveOrNull`, which will return a nullable version at the same time. Once the channel gets closed, we'll receive `null` in our `select`.

We can handle this null value in any way we want, for example, by making use of the `elvis` operator:

```
repeat(15) {
    val result = selectUnbiased<String> {
```

```
        p1.onReceiveOrNull {
            // Can throw my own exception
            it ?: throw RuntimeException()
        }
        p2.onReceiveOrNull {
            // Or supply default value
            it ?: "p2 closed"
        }
    }

    println(result)
}
```

Using that knowledge, we can drain both channels by skipping the null results:

```
var count = 0
while (count < 15) {
    val result = selectUnbiased<String?> {
        p1.onReceiveOrNull {
            it
        }
        p2.onReceiveOrNull {
            it
        }
    }

    if (result != null) {
        println(result)
        count++
    }
}
```

Sidekick channel

Up until now, we've only discussed the usages of select as a receiver. But we can also use select to send items to another channel.

Let's look at the following example:

```
val batman = actor<String> {
    for (c in this) {
        println("Batman is beating some sense into $c")
        delay(100)
    }
}
```

```
val robin = actor<String> {
    for (c in this) {
        println("Robin is beating some sense into $c")
        delay(250)
    }
}
```

We have a superhero and their sidekick as two actors. Since the superhero is more experienced, it usually takes them less time to beat the villain they're facing.

But in some cases, they still have their hands full, so a sidekick needs to step in.

We'll throw five villains at the pair with a few delays, and see how they fare:

```
val j = launch {
    for (c in listOf("Jocker", "Bane", "Penguin", "Riddler", "Killer
Croc")) {
        val result = select<Pair<String, String>> {
            batman.onSend(c) {
                Pair("Batman", c)
            }
            robin.onSend(c) {
                Pair("Robin", c)
            }
        }
        delay(90)
        println(result)
    }
}
```

It prints:

```
Batman is beating some sense into Jocker
(Batman, Jocker)
Robin is beating some sense into Bane
(Robin, Bane)
Batman is beating some sense into Penguin
(Batman, Penguin)
Batman is beating some sense into Riddler
(Batman, Riddler)
Robin is beating some sense into Killer Croc
(Robin, Killer Croc)
```

Notice that the type parameter for this select refers to what is returned from the block, and not what is being sent to the channels.

That's the reason we use `Pair<String, String>` here.

Deferred channel

The more you work with coroutines, the more you'll get used to await results. At some point, you'll start sending deferred values over channels.

We'll start by creating 10 async tasks. The first will delay for a long time, and others we delay for a short time:

```
val elements = 10
val deferredChannel = Channel<Deferred<Int>>(elements)

launch(CommonPool) {
    repeat(elements) { i ->
        println("$i sent")
        deferredChannel.send(async {
            delay(if (i == 0) 1000 else 10)
            i
        })
    }
}
```

We'll put all those results into a buffered channel.

Now we can read from this channel, and be using a second `select` block, and await the results:

```
val time = measureTimeMillis {
    repeat(elements) {
        val result = select<Int> {
            deferredChannel.onReceive {
                select {
                    it.onAwait { it }
                }
            }
        }
        println(result)
    }
}

println("Took ${time}ms")
```

Note that the resulting time is of the slowest task:

Took 1010ms

You can also use onAwait() as a stop signal for another channel.

For that, we'll create an async task that will complete in 600 ms:

```
val stop = async {
    delay(600)
    true
}
```

And, as in the previous example, we'll send 10 deferred values over the buffered channel:

```
val channel = Channel<Deferred<Int>>(10)

repeat(10) {i ->
    channel.send(async {
        delay(i * 100)
        i
    })
}
```

Then we'll wait for either a new value or a notification that the channel should be closed:

```
runBlocking {
    for (i in 1..10) {
        select<Unit> {
            stop.onAwait {
                channel.close()
            }
            channel.onReceive {
                println(it.await())
            }
        }
    }
}
```

This prints only six values out of ten, as expected, stopping after 600 ms have passed.

Summary

In this chapter, we covered various design patterns related to concurrency in Kotlin. Most of them are based on coroutines, channels, deferred values, or a combination.

Pipeline, **fan-in**, and **fan-out** help distribute work and collect the results. **Deferred values** are used as placeholders for something that would resolve at a later time. **Schedulers** help us manage resources, mainly threads that back up the coroutines. **Mutexes** and **Barriers** help control that concurrency.

Now you should understand the `select` block and how it can be combined with channels and deferred values efficiently.

In the next chapter, we'll discuss Kotlin's idioms, best practices, and some of the anti-patterns that emerged with the language.

10
Idioms and Anti-Patterns

This chapter discusses the best and worst practices in Kotlin. You'll learn what idiomatic Kotlin code should look like and which patterns to avoid.

After completing this chapter, you should be able to write more readable and maintainable Kotlin code, as well as avoid some common pitfalls.

In this chapter, we will cover the following topics:

- Let
- Apply
- Also
- Run
- With
- Instance checks
- Try-with-resources
- Inline functions
- Reified
- Constants
- Constructor overload
- Dealing with nulls
- Explicit async
- Validation
- Sealed, not enumerated
- More companions
- Scala function

Let

Usually, we use `let()` to do something only if the object is `not null`:

```
val sometimesNull = if (Random().nextBoolean()) "not null" else null

sometimesNull?.let {
    println("It was $it this time")
}
```

One common gotcha here is that `let()` by itself also works on nulls:

```
val alwaysNull = null

alwaysNull.let { // No null pointer there
    println("It was $it this time") // Always prints null
}
```

Don't forget the question mark, ?, when you use `let()` for null checks.

The return value of `let()` is not related to the type it operates on:

```
val numberReturned = justAString.let {
    println(it)
    it.length
}
```

This code will print `"string"` and return `Int` 6 as its length.

Apply

We have already discussed `apply()` in previous chapters. It returns the same object it operates on and sets the context to `this`. The most useful case for this function is setting the fields of a mutable object.

Think of how many times you had to create a class with an empty constructor, then call a lot of setters, one after another:

```
class JamesBond {
    lateinit var name: String
    lateinit var movie: String
    lateinit var alsoStarring: String
}
```

```
val agentJavaWay = JamesBond()
agentJavaWay.name = "Sean Connery"
agentJavaWay.movie = "Dr. No"
```

We can set only name and movie, but leave alsoStarring blank, like this:

```
val `007` = JamesBond().apply {
    this.name = "Sean Connery"
    this.movie = "Dr. No"
}

println(`007`.name)
```

Since the context is set to this, we can simplify it to the following nice syntax:

```
val `007` = JamesBond().apply {
    name = "Sean Connery"
    movie = "Dr. No"
}
```

This function is especially good when you work with Java classes that usually have a lot of setters.

Also

Single-expression functions are very nice and concise:

```
fun multiply(a: Int, b: Int): Int = a * b
```

But often, you have a single-statement function, that also needs to write to a log, for example.

You could write it the following way:

```
fun multiply(a: Int, b: Int): Int {
    val c = a * b
    println(c)
    return c
}
```

But then it's not a single statement function anymore, right?

And we also introduced another variable. To the rescue, `also()`:

```
fun multiply(a: Int, b: Int): Int = (a * b).also { println(it) }
```

This function will set results of the expression to `it` and return the result of the expression.

This is also useful when you want to have a side effect on a chain of calls:

```
val l = (1..100).toList()

l.filter{ it % 2 == 0 }
    .also { println(it) } // Prints, but doesn't change anything
    .map { it * it }
```

Run

Not related to threads in any way, `run()` is much like `let()`, but it sets the context to `this` instead of using `it`:

```
val justAString = "string"

val n = justAString.run {
    this.length
}
```

Usually, `this` could be omitted:

```
val n = justAString.run {
    length
}
```

It is mostly useful when you plan to call a number of methods on the same object, much like `apply()`.

The return result, unlike `apply()`, may be of a totally different type, though:

```
val year = JamesBond().run {
    name = "ROGER MOORE"
    movie = "THE MAN WITH THE GOLDEN GUN"
    1974 // <= Not JamesBond type
}
```

With

Unlike the other four scoping functions, `with()` is not an extension function.

This means you cannot do the following:

```
"scope".with { ... }
```

Instead, `with()` receives the object you want to scope as an argument:

```
with("scope") {
    println(this.length) // "this" set to the argument of with()
}
```

And as usual, we can omit `this`:

```
with("scope") {
    length
}
```

Just like `run()` and `let()`, you can return any result from `with()`.

Instance checks

Coming from Java, you may be inclined to check what type your object is using, `is`, and cast it using `as`:

```
interface Superhero
class Batman : Superhero {
    fun callRobin() {
        println("To the Bat-pole, Robin!")
    }
}

class Superman : Superhero {
    fun fly() {
        println("Up, up and away!")
    }
}

fun doCoolStuff(s : Superhero) {
    if (s is Superman) {
        (s as Superman).fly()
    }
    else if (s is Batman) {
```

```
        (a as Batman).callRobin()
    }
}
```

But as you may know, Kotlin has smart casts, so implicit casting, in this case, is not needed:

```
fun doCoolStuff(s : Superhero) {
    if (s is Superman) {
        s.fly()
    }
    else if (s is Batman) {
        s.callRobin()
    }
}
```

Moreover, in most cases, using `when()` while smart-casting produces cleaner code:

```
fun doCoolStuff(s : Superhero) {
    when(s) {
        is Superman -> s.fly()
        is Batman -> s.callRobin()
        else -> println("Unknown superhero")
    }
}
```

As a rule of thumb, you should avoid using casts and rely on smart casts most of the time:

```
// Superhero is clearly not a string
val superheroAsString = (s as String)
```

But if you absolutely must, there's also a safe cast operator:

```
val superheroAsString = (s as? String)
```

Try-with-resources

Java7 added the notion of `AutoCloseable` and the try-with-resources statement.

This statement allows us to provide a set of resources that would be automatically closed after the code is done with them. No more risk (or at least less risk) of forgetting to close a file.

Before Java7, that was a total mess:

```
BufferedReader br = null; // Nulls are bad, we know that
try {
    br = new BufferedReader(new FileReader("/some/peth"));
    System.out.println(br.readLine());
}
finally {
    if (br != null) { // Explicit check
        br.close(); // Boilerplate
    }
}
```

After Java7:

```
try (BufferedReader br = new BufferedReader(new FileReader("/some/peth")))
{
    System.out.println(br.readLine());
}
```

In Kotlin, the `this` statement is replaced with the `use()` function:

```
val br = BufferedReader(FileReader(""))

br.use {
    println(it.readLine())
}
```

Inline functions

You can think of inline functions as a copy/paste instruction for the compiler. Each time the compiler sees a call to a function marked with inline, it will replace the call with the `concrete` function body.

It makes sense to use the inline function only if it's a higher-order function that receives a lambda as one of its arguments:

```
inline fun doesntMakeSense(something: String) {
    println(something)
}
```

This is the most common use case where you would like to use `inline`:

```
inline fun makesSense(block: () -> String) {
    println("Before")
    println(block())
    println("After")
}
```

You call it as usual, with the block body:

```
makesSense {
    "Inlining"
}
```

But if you view the bytecode, you'll see it's actually translated to the lines produces and not to a function call:

```
println("Before")
println("Inlining")
println("After")
```

In the actual code, you'll see the following:

```
String var1 = "Before"; <- Inline function call
System.out.println(var1);
var1 = "Inlining";
System.out.println(var1);
var1 = "After";
System.out.println(var1);

var1 = "Before"; // <- Usual code
System.out.println(var1);
var1 = "Inlining";
System.out.println(var1);
var1 = "After";
System.out.println(var1);
```

Notice there's absolutely no difference between the two blocks.

Since the inline function is copy/paste, you shouldn't use it if you have more than a few lines of code. It would be more efficient to have it as a regular function.

Reified

Since the inline function is copied, we can get rid of one of the major JVM limitations–type erasure. After all, inside the function, we know exactly what type we're getting.

Let's look at the following example. You would like to create a generic function, which will receive a number but will print it only if it's of the same type as the function.

You can try writing something like this:

```
fun <T> printIfSameType(a: Number) {
    if (a is T) { // <== Error
        println(a)
    }
}
```

But this code won't compile with an error as follows:

Cannot check for instance of erased type: T

What we usually do in Java, in this case, is pass the class as an argument:

```
fun <T: Number> printIfSameType(clazz: KClass<T>, a: Number) {
    if (clazz.isInstance(a) ) {
        println(a)
    }
}
```

We can check this code by running the following two lines:

```
printIfSameType(Int::class, 1) // Print 1, as 1 is Int
printIfSameType(Int::class, 2L) // Prints nothing, as 2 is Long
```

This code has a few downsides:

- We had to use reflection, and for that, we had to include the `kotlin-reflect` library:

    ```
    compile group: 'org.jetbrains.kotlin', name: 'kotlin-reflect',
    version: '1.2.31'
    ```

- We cannot use the `is` operator and must use the `isInstance()` function instead.
- We must pass the correct class:

    ```
    clazz: KClass<T>
    ```

Instead, we can use a `reified` function:

```
inline fun <reified T> printIfSameTypeReified(a: Number) {
    if (a is T) {
        println(a)
    }
}
```

We can test that our code still works as expected:

```
printIfSameTypeReified<Int>(3)   // Prints 3, as 3 is Int
printIfSameTypeReified<Int>(4L)  // Prints nothing, as 4 is Long
printIfSameTypeReified<Long>(5)  // Prints nothing, as 5 is Int
printIfSameTypeReified<Long>(6L) // Prints 6, as 6 is Long
```

We get all the benefits of the language this way:

- No need for another dependency
- Clear method signature
- Ability to use the `is` construct

Of course, the same rules as regular inline functions apply. This code would be replicated, so it shouldn't be too large.

Consider another case regarding function overloading:

```
fun printList(list: List<Int>) {
    println("This is a lit of Ints")
    println(list)
}

fun printList(list: List<Long>) {
    println("This is a lit of Longs")
    println(list)
}
```

This won't compile because there's a platform declaration clash. Both have the same signature in terms of JVM: `printList(list: List)`.

But with `reified`, we can achieve this:

```
const val int = 1
const val long = 1L
inline fun <reified T : Any> printList(list: List<T>) {
    when {
        int is T -> println("This is a list of Ints")
        long is T -> println("This is a list of Longs")
```

```
        else -> println("This is a list of something else")
    }

    println(list)
}
```

Constants

Since everything in Java is an object (unless you're a primitive type), we're used to putting all the constants inside our objects as static members.

And since Kotlin has companion objects, we usually try putting them there:

```
class MyClass {
    companion object {
        val MY_CONST = "My Const"
    }
}
```

This will work, but you should remember that companion object is an object, after all.

So, this will be translated to the following code, more or less:

```
public final class Spock {
    @NotNull
    private static final String MY_CONST = "My Const";
    public static final Spock.Companion Companion = new
Spock.Companion(...);

    public static final class Companion {
        @NotNull
        public final String getMY_CONST() {
            return MyClass.MY_CONST;
        }

        private Companion() {
        }
    }
}
```

And the call to our constant looks like this:

```
String var1 = Spock.Companion.getSENSE_OF_HUMOR();
System.out.println(var1);
```

So, we have our class, Spock, inside of which we have another class. But what we wanted was only static final String.

Let's now mark this value as constant:

```
class Spock {
    companion object {
        const val SENSE_OF_HUMOR = "None"
    }
}
```

Here are the bytecode changes:

```
public final class Spock {
    @NotNull
    public static final String SENSE_OF_HUMOR = "NONE";
    public static final Spock.Companion Companion = new
Spock.Companion(...);
    )
    public static final class Companion {
        private Companion() {
        }
            ...
    }
}
```

And here is the call:

```
String var1 = "NONE";
System.out.println(var1);
```

Notice that there's no call to this constant at all since the compiler already inlined its value for us. After all, it's constant.

If all you need is a constant, you can also set it up outside of any class:

```
const val SPOCK_SENSE_OF_HUMOR = "NONE"
```

And if you need namespacing, you can wrap it in an object:

```
object SensesOfHumor {
    const val SPOCK = "NONE"
}
```

Constructor overload

In Java, we're used to having overloaded constructors:

```
class MyClass {
    private final String a;
    private final Integer b;
    public MyClass(String a) {
        this(a, 1);
    }

    public MyClass(String a, Integer b) {
        this.a = a;
        this.b = b;
    }
}
```

We can simulate the same behavior in Kotlin:

```
class MyClass(val a: String, val b: Int, val c: Long) {
    constructor(a: String, b: Int) : this(a, b, 0)
    constructor(a: String) : this(a, 1)
    constructor() : this("Default")
}
```

But it's usually better to have default parameter values and named arguments instead:

```
class BetterClass(val a: String = "Default",
                  val b: Int = 1,
                  val c: Long = 0)
```

Dealing with nulls

Nulls are unavoidable, especially if you work with Java libraries or get data from a database.

But you can check for null the Java way:

```
// Will return "String" half of the time, and null the other half
val stringOrNull: String? = if (Random().nextBoolean()) "String" else null

// Java-way check
if (stringOrNull != null) {
    println(stringOrNull.length)
}
```

Or in a shorter form, with the `Elvis` operator. If the length is not null, this operator will return its value. Otherwise, it will return the default value we supplied, zero in this case:

```
val alwaysLength = stringOrNull?.length ?: 0

println(alwaysLength) // Will print 6 or 0, but never null
```

If you have a nested object, you can chain those checks:

```
data class Json(
        val User: Profile?
)

data class Profile(val firstName: String?,
                   val lastName: String?)

val json: Json? = Json(Profile(null, null))

println(json?.User?.firstName?.length)
```

Finally, you can use the `let()` block for those checks:

```
println(json?.let {
    it.User?.let {
        it.firstName?.length
    }
})
```

If you want to get rid of the `it()` everywhere, you can use run:

```
println(json?.run {
    User?.run {
        firstName?.length
    }
})
```

By all means, do try to avoid the unsafe `!!` null operator:

```
println(json!!.User!!.firstName!!.length)
```

This will result in `KotlinNullPointerException`.

Explicit async

As you saw in the previous chapter, in Kotlin it is very easy to introduce concurrency:

```
fun getName() = async {
    delay(100)
    "Ruslan"
}
```

But that concurrency may be unexpected behavior to the user of the function, as they may expect a simple value:

```
println("Name: ${getName()}")
```

It prints:

Name: DeferredCoroutine{Active}@...

Of course, what's missing here is `await()`:

```
println("Name: ${getName().await()}")
```

But it would have been a lot more obvious if we'd named our function accordingly:

```
fun getNameAsync() = async {
    delay(100)
    "Ruslan"
}
```

As a rule, you should establish some kind of convention to distinguish async functions from regular ones.

Validation

How many times did you have to write code like this:

```
fun setCapacity(cap: Int) {
    if (cap < 0) {
        throw IllegalArgumentException()
    }
    ...
}
```

Instead, you can check arguments with `require()`:

```
fun setCapacity(cap: Int) {
    require(cap > 0)
}
```

This makes the code a lot more fluent.

You can use `require()` to check for nested nulls:

```
fun printNameLength(p: Profile) {
    require(p.firstName != null)
}
```

But there's also `requireNotNull()` for that:

```
fun printNameLength(p: Profile) {
    requireNotNull(p.firstName)
}
```

Use `check()` to validate the state of your object. This is useful when you provide some object that the user may not have set up correctly:

```
private class HttpClient {
    var body: String? = null
    var url: String = ""

    fun postRequest() {
        check(body != null) {
            "Body must be set in POST requests"
        }
    }
    fun getRequest() {
        // This one is fine without body
    }
}
```

And again, there's a shortcut for `null`: `checkNotNull()`.

Sealed, not enumerated

Coming from Java, you may be tempted to overload your `enum` with functionality:

```
// Java code
enum PizzaOrderStatus {
```

```
ORDER_RECEIVED,
PIZZA_BEING_MADE,
OUT_FOR_DELIVERY,
COMPLETED;


public PizzaOrderStatus nextStatus() {
    switch (this) {
        case ORDER_RECEIVED: return PIZZA_BEING_MADE;
        case PIZZA_BEING_MADE: return OUT_FOR_DELIVERY;
        case OUT_FOR_DELIVERY: return COMPLETED;
        case COMPLETED:return COMPLETED;
    }
  }
}
```

Instead, you can use the `sealed` class:

```
sealed class PizzaOrderStatus(protected val orderId: Int) {
    abstract fun nextStatus() : PizzaOrderStatus
    class OrderReceived(orderId: Int) : PizzaOrderStatus(orderId) {
        override fun nextStatus(): PizzaOrderStatus {
            return PizzaBeingMade(orderId)
        }
    }

    class PizzaBeingMade(orderId: Int) : PizzaOrderStatus(orderId) {
        override fun nextStatus(): PizzaOrderStatus {
            return OutForDelivery(orderId)
        }
    }

    class OutForDelivery(orderId: Int) : PizzaOrderStatus(orderId) {
        override fun nextStatus(): PizzaOrderStatus {
            return Completed(orderId)
        }
    }

    class Completed(orderId: Int) : PizzaOrderStatus(orderId) {
        override fun nextStatus(): PizzaOrderStatus {
            return this
        }
    }
}
```

The benefit of this approach is that we can now pass data around along with the status:

```
var status: PizzaOrderStatus = OrderReceived(123)

while (status !is Completed) {
    status = when (status) {
        is OrderReceived -> status.nextStatus()
        is PizzaBeingMade -> status.nextStatus()
        is OutForDelivery -> status.nextStatus()
        is Completed -> status
    }
}
```

In general, sealed classes are good if you want to have data associated with a state.

More companions

You are limited to having only one companion object in your class:

```
class A {
    companion {
    }
    companion {
    }
}
```

But you can have as many objects in your class as you want:

```
class A {
    object B {
    }
    object C {
    }
}
```

This is sometimes used to produce namespacing. Namespacing is important because it provides you with better naming conventions. Think about having cases when you created classes such as `SimpleJsonParser`, which inherits from `JsonParser`, which inherits from `Parser`. You could convert this structure to `Json.Parser`, for example, which is much more concise and practical, as Kotlin code should be.

Scala functions

Developers coming into Kotlin from Scala may sometimes define their function this way:

```
fun hello() = {
    "hello"
}
```

Calling this function won't print what you expect:

```
println("Say ${hello()}")
```

It prints the following:

```
 Say () -> kotlin.String
```

What we're missing is the second set of parentheses:

```
println("Say ${hello()()}")
```

It prints the following:

Say hello

That's because the single-expression definition could be translated into:

```
fun hello(): () -> String {
    return {
        "hello"
    }
}
```

It could be further translated into:

```
fun helloExpandedMore(): () -> String {
    return fun(): String {
        return "hello"
    }
}
```

Now you can see where that function came from, at least.

Summary

In this chapter, we reviewed best practices in Kotlin, as well as some of the caveats of the language. Now you should be able to write more idiomatic code that is also performant and maintainable.

You should make use of scoping functions, but make sure not to overuse them, as they may make the code confusing, especially for those newer to the language.

Be sure to handle nulls and type casts correctly, with `let()`, the `Elvis` operator, and smart casts that the language provides.

In the next and final chapter, we'll put those skills to use by writing a real-life microservice using everything we've learned.

11
Reactive Microservices with Kotlin

In this chapter, we'll put the skills we've learned so far to use by building a microservice using the Kotlin programming language. We also want this microservice to be reactive, and to be as close to real life as possible. For that, we'll use Vert.x framework, the benefits of which we'll list in the next section.

You're probably tired of creating to-do or shopping lists.

So, instead, the microservice will be for a *cat shelter*. The microservice should be able to do the following:

- Supply an endpoint we can ping to check whether the service is up and running
- List cats currently in the shelter
- Provide us with a means to add new cats

What you'll need to get started:

- JDK 1.8 or later
- IntelliJ IDEA
- Gradle 4.2 or later
- PostgreSQL 9.4 or later

This chapter will assume that you have `PostgreSQL` already installed and that you have basic knowledge of working with it. If you don't, please refer to the official documentation: `https://www.postgresql.org/docs/9.4/static/tutorial-install.html`.

In this chapter, we will cover the following topics:

- Getting started with Vert.x
- Handling requests
- Testing
- Working with databases
- EventBus

Getting started with Vert.x

The framework we'll be using for our microservice is called **Vert.x**. It's a reactive framework that shares much in common with **reactive extensions**, which we discussed in Chapter 7, *Staying Reactive*. It's asynchronous and non-blocking.

Let's understand what this means by using a concrete example.

We'll start with a new Kotlin Gradle project. From your IntelliJ IDEA, open **File | New | Project**, and choose **Gradle | Kotlin** in the **New Project** wizard. Give your project a GroupId (I chose me.soshin) and an ArtifactId (catsShelter in my case).

 Gradle is a build tool, similar to Maven and Ant. It has a nice syntax and compiles your projects in an optimised way. You can read about it more here: https://gradle.org/.

On the next screen, choose **Use auto-import** and **Create directories for empty content roots**, then click **Finish**.

Next, add the following dependencies to your build.gradle.

```
dependencies {
    def $vertx_version = '3.5.1'
    ...
    compile group: 'io.vertx', name: 'vertx-core', version: $vertx_version
    compile group: 'io.vertx', name: 'vertx-web', version: $vertx_version
    compile group: 'io.vertx', name: 'vertx-lang-kotlin', version:
$vertx_version
    compile group: 'io.vertx', name: 'vertx-lang-kotlin-coroutines',
version: $vertx_version
}
```

The following is an explanation of each dependency:

- `vertx-core` is the core library
- `vertx-web` is needed, since we want our service to be REST based
- `vertx-lang-kotlin` provides idiomatic ways to write Kotlin code with Vert.x
- Finally, `vertx-lang-kotlin-coroutines` integrates with the coroutines we discussed in detail in `Chapter 9`, *Designed for Concurrency*

Note that we defined a variable to specify which version of Vert.x we should use. The latest stable version to date is 3.5.1, but by the time you read this book, it will be 3.5.2 or even 3.6.0.

As a general rule, all Vert.x libraries should be the same version, and that's when the variable becomes useful.

Create a file called `Main.kt` in the `src/main/kotlin` folder with the following content:

```
fun main(vararg args: String) {
    val vertx = Vertx.vertx()

    vertx.createHttpServer().requestHandler{ req ->
            req.response().end("OK")
        }.listen(8080)
}
```

That's all you need to start a web server that will respond *OK* when you open `http://localhost:8080` in your browser.

Now let's understand what actually happens here. We create a Vert.x instance using the **Factory Method** from `Chapter 3`, *Understanding Structural Patterns*.

Handler is just a simple listener, or a subscriber. If you don't remember how it works, check `Chapter 4`, *Getting Familiar with Behavioral Patterns*, for an **Observable** design pattern. In our case, it will be called for each new request. That's the asynchronous nature of Vert.x in action.

Notice that `requestHandler()` is a function that receives a block. Like any other idiomatic Kotlin code, you don't need the parentheses.

If you are using an IDE such as IntelliJ IDEA, you can run it directly. An alternative would be to add the following lines to your `build.gradle`:

```
apply plugin: 'application'
mainClassName = "com.gett.MainKt"
```

And then you can simply start it with the following:

```
./gradlew run
```

Another option would be to use `VertxGradlePlugin` (https://github.com/jponge/vertx-gradle-plugin), which will do the same thing.

Routing

Notice that no matter which URL we specify, we always get the same result.

Of course, that's not what we want to achieve. Let's start by adding the most basic endpoint, which will only tell us that the service is up and running.

For that, we'll use `Router`:

```
val vertx = Vertx.vertx() // Was here before
val router = Router.router(vertx)
...
```

`Router` lets you specify handlers for different HTTP methods and URLs.

But, by default, it doesn't support coroutines. Let's fix that by creating an extension function:

```
fun Route.asyncHandler(fn : suspend (RoutingContext) -> Unit) {
    handler { ctx ->
        launch(ctx.vertx().dispatcher()) {
            try {
                fn(ctx)
            } catch(e: Exception) {
                ctx.fail(e)
            }
        }
    }
}
```

If you are familiar with modern JavaScript, this is similar to `async() => {}`.

Now we can use this new extension method:

```
router.get("/alive").asyncHandler {
    // Some response comes here
    // We now can use any suspending function in this context
}
```

We saw how we return a flat text response in the very first example. So, let's return JSON instead. Most real-life applications use JSON for communication.

Add the following lines to your handler:

```
...
val json = json {
    obj (
        "alive" to true
    )
}
it.respond(json.toString())
...
```

Yet another extension function we declare is `respond()`. It looks as follows:

```
fun RoutingContext.respond(responseBody: String = "", status: Int = 200) {
    this.response()
            .setStatusCode(status)
            .end(responseBody)
}
```

Now connect your router to the server.

You can do that by replacing the previous server instantiation with the following line:

```
vertx.createHttpServer().
    requestHandler(router::accept).listen(8080)
```

Now all routing will be handled by `Router`.

You can open `http://localhost:8080/alive` in your browser and make sure that you get `{"alive": true}` as a response.

Congratulations! You've managed to create your first route that returns a JSON. From now on, whenever you're not sure whether your application is up and running, you can simply check it using this URL. This becomes even more important when you use a load balancer, which needs to know how many applications are available at any time.

Handling requests

Our next task is adding the first cat to our virtual shelter.

It should be a `POST` request, where the body of the request may look something like this:
`{"name": "Binky", "age": 4}`.

If you are familiar with tools such as **curl** or **Postman** to issue `POST` requests, that's great. If not, we'll write a test in the next section that will check exactly that scenario.

The first thing we'll need to do is add the following line after we initialize our router:

```
router.route().handler(BodyHandler.create())
```

This will tell Vert.x to parse the request body into JSON for any request. Another way would be to use `router.route("/*")`.

Now, let's figure out what our URL should look like. It is good practice to have our API URLs versioned, so we would like it to be as follows:

```
api/v1/cats
```

So, we can assume the following:

- `GET api/v1/cats` will return all cats we have in our shelter
- `POST api/v1/cats` will add a new cat
- `GET api/v1/cats/34` will return a cat with `ID=34` if it exists or 404 otherwise

Having figured that out, we can progress as follows:

```
router.post("/api/v1/cats").asyncHandler { ctx ->
    // Some code of adding a cat comes here
}
router.get("/api/v1/cats").asyncHandler { ctx ->
    // Code for getting all the cats
}
```

The last endpoint will need to receive a path argument. We use semicolon notation for that:

```
router.get("/api/v1/cats/:id").asyncHandler { ctx ->
    // Fetches specific cat
}
```

Verticles

Now come across a problem, though. Our code resides in the `Main.kt` file, which grows bigger and bigger. We can start splitting it by using verticles.

You can think of a verticle as a lightweight actor. Let's see an example; look at the following code:

```
class ServerVerticle: CoroutineVerticle() {

    override suspend fun start() {
        val router = router()
vertx.createHttpServer().requestHandler(router::accept).listen(8080)
    }

    private fun router(): Router {
        val router = Router.router(vertx)
        // Our router code comes here now
        ...
        return router
    }
}
```

Now we need to start this verticle. There are different ways of doing that, but the simplest way is to pass the instance of this class to the `deployVerticle()` method:

```
vertx.deployVerticle(ServerVerticle())
```

Now our code is split into two files, `ServerVerticle.kt` and `Main.kt`.

Notice, though, how `/api/v1/cats/` is repeated every time. Isn't there a way to remove that redundancy? Actually, there is. And it's called **subrouter**.

Subrouting

We'll leave the `/alive` endpoint as it is, but we'll extract all the other endpoints into a separate function:

```
private fun apiRouter(): Router {
    val router = Router.router(vertx)

    router.post("/cats").asyncHandler { ctx ->
        ctx.respond(status=501)
    }
    router.get("/cats").asyncHandler { ctx ->
```

```
    . . .
}
router.get("/cats/:id").asyncHandler { ctx ->
    . . .
}
return router
}
```

There's a more fluent way to define it, but we left it that way as it is more readable.

Much as we supplied our main router to the Vert.x server instance, we now supply our subrouter to the main router as follows:

```
router.mountSubRouter("/api/v1", apiRouter())
```

Keeping our code clean and well separated is very important.

Testing

Before we continue to add our cats to the database, let's first write some tests to make sure that everything works correctly so far.

For that, we'll use the **TestNG** test framework. You can also use **JUnit** or **VertxUnit** for the same purpose.

Start by adding the following line to the **dependencies** part of your `build.gradle`:

```
testCompile group: 'org.testng', name: 'testng', version: '6.11'
```

Now we'll create our first test. It should be located under `/src/test/kotlin/<your_package>`.

The basic structure of all the integration tests looks something like this:

```
class ServerVerticleTest {
    // Usually one instance of VertX is more than enough
    val vertx = Vertx.vertx()

    @BeforeClass
    fun setUp() {
        // You want to start your server once
        startServer()
    }

    @AfterClass
```

```
fun tearDown() {
    // And you want to stop your server once
    vertx.close()
}

@Test
fun testAlive() {
    // Here you assert something
}

// More tests come here
...
}
```

A good trick is to name your tests using Kotlin backtick notation.

You could name your tests like this:

```
@Test
fun testAlive() {
    ...
}
```

But it is better to name your tests like this:

```
@Test
fun `Tests that alive works`() {
    ...
}
```

Now we want to issue an actual HTTP call to our /alive endpoint, for example, and check the response code. For that, we'll use the Vert.x web client.

Add it to your build.gradle dependencies section:

```
compile group: 'io.vertx', name: 'vertx-web-client', version:
$vertx_version
```

If you plan to use it only in tests, you can specify testCompile instead of compile. But WebClient is so useful you'll probably end up using it in your code anyway.

Helper methods

We'll create two helper functions in our test, called `get()` and `post()`, which will issue `GET` and `POST` requests to our test server.

We'll start with `get()`:

```
private fun get(path: String): HttpResponse<Buffer> {
    val d1 = CompletableDeferred<HttpResponse<Buffer>>()

    val client = WebClient.create(vertx)
    client.get(8080, "localhost", path).send {
        d1.complete(it.result())
    }

    return runBlocking {
        d1.await()
    }
}
```

The second method, `post()`, will look very similar, but it will also have a request body parameter:

```
private fun post(path: String, body: String = ""): HttpResponse<Buffer> {
    val d1 = CompletableDeferred<HttpResponse<Buffer>>()

    val client = WebClient.create(vertx)
    client.post(8080, "localhost", path).sendBuffer(Buffer.buffer(body), {
res ->
        d1.complete(res.result())
    })

    return runBlocking {
        d1.await()
    }
}
```

Both of those functions use coroutines and the default parameter values Kotlin provides.

You should write your own helper functions or alter those according to your needs.

Another helper function that we'll need is `startServer()`, which we already mentioned in `@BeforeClass`. It should look something like this:

```
private fun startServer() {
    val d1 = CompletableDeferred<String>()
    vertx.deployVerticle(ServerVerticle(), {
```

```
        d1.complete("OK")
    })
    runBlocking {
        println("Server started")
        d1.await()
    }
}
```

We'll need two new extension functions for our convenience. Those functions will convert the server response to JSON:

```
private fun <T> HttpResponse<T>.asJson(): JsonNode {
    return this.bodyAsBuffer().asJson()
}

private fun Buffer.asJson(): JsonNode {
    return ObjectMapper().readTree(this.toString())
}
```

Now we're all set to write our first test:

```
@Test
fun `Tests that alive works`() {
    val response = get("/alive")
    assertEquals(response.statusCode(), 200)

    val body = response.asJson()
    assertEquals(body["alive"].booleanValue(), true)
}
```

Run `./gradlew test` to check that this test passes.

Next, we'll write another test; this time for the cat's creation endpoint.

At first, it will fail:

```
@Test
fun `Makes sure cat can be created`() {
    val response = post("/api/v1/cats",
                """
                {
                    "name": "Binky",
                    "age": 5
                }
                """)

    assertEquals(response.statusCode(), 201)
    val body = response.asJson()
```

```
assertNotNull(body["id"])
assertEquals(body["name"].textValue(), "Binky")
assertEquals(body["age"].intValue(), 5)
}
```

Note that our server returns the status code `501 Not Implemented`, and doesn't return the `cat` ID.

We'll be fixing that in the next section when we discuss persistence in a database.

Working with databases

We won't be able to progress much further without the ability to save our objects, namely cats, into some kind of persistent storage.

For that, we'll need to connect to the database first.

Add the following two lines to your `build.gradle` dependencies section:

```
compile group: 'org.postgresql', name: 'postgresql', version: '42.2.2'
compile group: 'io.vertx', name: 'vertx-jdbc-client', version:
$vertx_version
```

The first line of code fetches the `PostgreSQL` driver. The second one adds the Vert.x JDBC client, which allows Vert.x, having the driver, to connect to any database that supports JDBC.

Managing configuration

Now we want to hold database configuration somewhere. For local development, it may be fine to have those configurations hardcoded.

When we connect to the database, we need to specify the following parameters at the very least:

- Username
- Password
- Host
- Database name

Where should we store them?

One option is of course to hardcode those values. That would be fine for a local environment, but what about when deploying this service somewhere?

You'll go, I cant come! XDSpringBoot do, or we could attempt to read them from the environment variables. Anyway, we'll need an object that would encapsulate this logic, as shown in the following code:

```
object Config {
    object Db {
        val username = System.getenv("DATABASE_USERNAME") ?: "postgres"
        val password = System.getenv("DATABASE_PASSWORD") ?: ""
        val database = System.getenv("DATABASE_NAME") ?: "cats_db"
        val host = System.getenv("DATABASE_HOST") ?: ""

        override fun toString(): String {
            return mapOf("username" to username,
                    "password" to password,
                    "database" to database,
                    "host" to host).toString()
        }
    }
    override fun toString(): String {
        return mapOf(
                "Db" to Db
        ).toString()
    }
}
```

That's of course only one approach you could take.

We now will create `JDBCClient` by using this configuration code:

```
fun CoroutineVerticle.getDbClient(): JDBCClient {
    val postgreSQLClientConfig = JsonObject(
            "url" to
"jdbc:postgresql://${Config.Db.host}:5432/${Config.Db.database}",
            "username" to Config.Db.username,
            "password" to Config.Db.password)
    return JDBCClient.createShared(vertx, postgreSQLClientConfig)
}
```

Here, we chose an extension function that will work on all `CoroutineVerticles`.

To simplify working with the `JDBCClient`, we'll add a method called `query()` to it:

```
fun JDBCClient.query(q: String, vararg params: Any): Deferred<JsonObject> {
    val deferred = CompletableDeferred<JsonObject>()
    this.getConnection { conn ->
        conn.handle({
            result().queryWithParams(q, params.toJsonArray(), { res ->
                res.handle({
                    deferred.complete(res.result().toJson())
                }, {
                    deferred.completeExceptionally(res.cause())
                })
            })
        }, {
            deferred.completeExceptionally(conn.cause())
        })
    }

    return deferred
}
```

We'll also add the `toJsonArray()` method since that's what our `JDBCClient` works with:

```
private fun <T> Array<T>.toJsonArray(): JsonArray {
    val json = JsonArray()

    for (e in this) {
        json.add(e)
    }

    return json
}
```

Note here how Kotlin generics are being used to simplify the conversion while *staying type-safe*.

And we'll add a `handle()` function, which will provide us with a simple API to handle asynchronous errors:

```
inline fun <T> AsyncResult<T>.handle(success: AsyncResult<T>.() -> Unit,
failure: () -> Unit) {
    if (this.succeeded()) {
        success()
    }
    else {
```

```
            this.cause().printStackTrace()
            failure()
        }
    }
```

To make sure everything works correctly, we'll add a check to our /alive route:

```
val router = Router.router(vertx)
val dbClient = getDbClient()
...
router.get("/alive").asyncHandler {
    val dbAlive = dbClient.query("select true as alive")
    val json = json {
        obj (
                "alive" to true,
                // This is JSON, but we can access it as an array
                "db" to dbAlive.await()["rows"]
        )
    }
    it.respond(json)
}
```

The lines you need to add are marked in bold.

After adding those lines and opening http://localhost:8080/alive you should get the following JSON code:

```
{"alive":true, "db":[{"alive":true}]}
```

Managing the database

Of course, our test doesn't work. That's because we haven't created our database yet. Make sure you run the following line in your command line:

```
$ createdb cats_db
```

After we have made sure that our database is up and running, let's implement our first real endpoint.

We'll keep our SQL nicely separated from the actual code. Add this to your ServerVerticle:

```
private val insert = """insert into cats (name, age)
            |values (?, ?::integer) RETURNING *""".trimMargin()
```

We use multiline strings here, with | and `trimMargin()` to re-align them.

Now use the following code to call this query:

```
...
val db = getDbClient()
router.post("/cats").asyncHandler { ctx ->
    db.queryWithParams(insert, ctx.bodyAsJson.toCat(), {
        it.handle({
            // We'll always have one result here, since it's our row
            ctx.respond(it.result().rows[0].toString(), 201)
        }, {
            ctx.respond(status=500)
        })
    })
}
```

Notice that we didn't print the error anywhere. That's because we defined the `handle()` function to do that.

We also defined our own function that parses the request body, which is `JsonObject`, to `JsonArray`, which is expected by the `JDBCClient`:

```
private fun JsonObject.toCat() = JsonArray().apply {
    add(this@toCat.getString("name"))
    add(this@toCat.getInteger("age"))
}
```

Notice that we have two different versions of `this` here. One refers to the inner scope of the `apply()` function. The other refers to the outer scope of the `toCat()` function. To refer to outer scopes, we use the `@scopeName` notation.

As you can see, extension functions are extremely powerful tools for cleaning up your code.

When you run our test again, you'll notice it still fails, but with a different error code now. That's because we didn't create our table yet. Let's do it now. There are a few ways to do this, but the most convenient way would be to simply run the following command:

```
psql -c "create table cats (id bigserial primary key, name varchar(20), age
integer)" cats_db
```

Run your test again to make sure it passes.

EventBus

This is the second time we have stumbled upon the same problem: our classes get bigger and bigger, which we would usually like to avoid as much as possible.

What if we split this creation of cats logic into a separate file yet again? Let's call it `CatVerticle.kt`.

But then we need a way for `ServerVerticle` to communicate with `CatVerticle`. In frameworks such as **SpringBoot**, you would use **dependency injection** for that purpose. But what about reactive frameworks?

Consumer

To solve communication problems, Vert.x uses **EventBus**. It's an implementation of the **Observable** design pattern we discussed in Chapter 4, *Getting Familiar with Behavioral Patterns*. Any verticle can send a message over the event bus, choosing between these two modes:

- `send()` will send a message to only one subscriber
- `publish()` will send a message to all subscribers

No matter which method is used to send the message, you subscribe to it using the `consumer()` method on the EventBus:

```
const val CATS = "cats:get"

class CatVerticle : CoroutineVerticle() {
    override suspend fun start() {
        val db = getDbClient()
        vertx.eventBus().consumer<JsonObject>(CATS) { req ->
            ...
        }
    }
}
```

The type specifies which object we expect to receive our message. In this case, it's `JsonObject`. Constant `CATS` is the key we subscribe for. It can be any string. By using a namespace, we ensure that there won't be a collision in the future. If we were to add dogs to our shelter, we would use another constant with another namespace. For example:

```
const val DOGS  = "dogs:get" // Just an example, don't copy it
```

Now we add the following two queries, which are just multiline string constants:

```
private const val QUERY_ALL = """select * from cats"""
class CatVerticle : CoroutineVerticle() {
    private val QUERY_WITH_ID = """select * from cats
                    where id = ?::integer""".trimIndent()
...
}
```

Why are we putting one inside the class and the other outside it?

QUERY_ALL is a short query and it fits on one line. We can allow ourselves to make it a constant. On the other hand, QUERY_WITH_ID is a longer query and it requires some indentation. Since we remove the indentation only at runtime, we can't make it a constant. So, instead, we use a member value. In real-life projects, most of your queries will probably have to be private values. But it's important to know the difference between the two approaches.

And we populate our consumer with the following code:

```
...
try {
    val body = req.body()
    val id: Int? = body["id"]
    val result = if (id != null) {
        db.query(QUERY_WITH_ID, id)
    } else {
        db.query(QUERY_ALL)
    }
    launch {
        req.reply(result.await())
    }
}
catch (e: Exception) {
    req.fail(0, e.message)
}
...
```

If we got a cat ID in the request, we fetch this specific cat. Otherwise, we fetch all the cats that are available.

We use launch() because we want to await() the result, and we don't have any return value.

Producer

What's left is only to call the cat from the `ServerVerticle`. For that, we'll add another method to our `CoroutineVerticle`:

```
fun <T> CoroutineVerticle.send(address: String,
                               message: T,
                               callback: (AsyncResult<Message<T>>) -> Unit)
{
    this.vertx.eventBus().send(address, message, callback)
}
```

Then we can handle our request like this:

```
...
router.get("/cats").asyncHandler { ctx ->
    send(CATS, ctx.queryParams().toJson()) {
        it.handle({
            val responseBody = it.result().body()
            ctx.respond(responseBody.get<JsonArray>("rows").toString())
        }, {
            ctx.respond(status=500)
        })
    }
}
...
```

Notice that we're reusing the same constant we defined earlier, called `CATS`.

That way, we can easily check who can send this event and who consumes it. If it's successful, we'll return a JSON. Otherwise, we'll return an HTTP error code.

Another method that we add is `toJson()` on `MultiMap`. `MultiMap` is an object that holds our query parameters:

```
private fun MultiMap.toJson(): JsonObject {
    val json = JsonObject()

    for (k in this.names()) {
        json.put(k, this[k])
    }

    return json
}
```

To make sure everything works as expected, let's create two more tests for our new endpoints.

Just don't forget to add the following line to your `Main.kt` and to the `startServer()` function in your tests:

```
...
vertx.deployVerticle(CatVerticle())
...
```

More testing

Now add the following basic test:

```
@Test
fun `Make sure that all cats are returned`() {
    val response = get("/api/v1/cats")
    assertEquals(response.statusCode(), 200)

    val body = response.asJson()

    assertTrue(body.size() > 0)
}
```

To make sure you understand how everything works together, here are some more assignments you may wish to do:

1. Move the logic of adding a new cat to the `CatVerticle`.
2. Implement getting a single cat. Notice how the code is very similar to the one that gets all the cats? Refactor it to use a local function, a cool feature in Kotlin, which we have already discussed.
3. Implement deletion and update the cat, following the same principles.

Summary

This chapter put together everything we've learned about Kotlin design patterns and idioms, to produce an extensible microservice. And, thanks to Vert.x, it's also reactive, which makes it extremely scalable. It also has tested in place, as any real-world application should.

In our application, classes are divided by domains, as opposed to layers, in the usual MVC architecture. A minimal unit of work in Vert.x is called a verticle, and verticles communicate using EventBus.

Our API follows all of REST's best practices: using HTTP verbs and meaningful paths to resources and consuming and producing JSON.

You can apply the same principles to any other real application you're going to write, and we do hope you'll choose Vert.x and Kotlin to do so.

Other Books You May Enjoy

If you enjoyed this book, you may be interested in these other books by Packt:

Kotlin Blueprints
Ashish Belagali

ISBN: 9781788390804

- See how Kotlin's power and versatility make it a great choice to create applications across various platforms, and how it delivers business and technology benefits
- Write a robust web applications using Kotlin with Spring Boot
- Write Android applications with ease using Kotlin
- Write rich desktop applications in Kotlin
- Learn how Kotlin can generate Javascript and how this can be used on client side and server side development
- Understand how native applications can be written with Kotlin/Native
- Learn the practical aspects of programming in each of the applications

Mastering Android Development with Kotlin

Miloš Vasić

ISBN: 9781788473699

- Understand the basics of Android development with Kotlin
- Get to know the key concepts in Android development
- See how to create modern mobile applications for the Android platform
- Adjust your application's look and feel
- Know how to persist and share application database
- Work with Services and other concurrency mechanisms
- Write effective tests
- Migrate an existing Java-based project to Kotlin

Leave a review - let other readers know what you think

Please share your thoughts on this book with others by leaving a review on the site that you bought it from. If you purchased the book from Amazon, please leave us an honest review on this book's Amazon page. This is vital so that other potential readers can see and use your unbiased opinion to make purchasing decisions, we can understand what our customers think about our products, and our authors can see your feedback on the title that they have worked with Packt to create. It will only take a few minutes of your time, but is valuable to other potential customers, our authors, and Packt. Thank you!

Index

www.ingramcontent.com/pod-product-compliance
Lightning Source LLC
LaVergne TN
LVHW081517050326
832903LV00025B/1525